Philosophy of Law

PRINCETON FOUNDATIONS OF CONTEMPORARY PHILOSOPHY

Scott Soames, *Series Editor*

Philosophical Logic by JOHN P. BURGESS
Philosophy of Language by SCOTT SOAMES

PHILOSOPHY OF LAW

Andrei Marmor

PRINCETON UNIVERSITY PRESS
PRINCETON AND OXFORD

Marmor, Andrei.
    Philosophy of law / Andrei Marmor.
        p. cm. — (The Princeton series in the foundations of contemporary
philosophy)
    Includes bibliographical references and index.
    ISBN 978-0-691-14167-1 (alk. paper)
    1. Law—Philosophy. I. Title.
    K231.M375 2011
    340'.1—dc22   2010026005

British Library Cataloging-in-Publication Data is available

This book has been composed in Minion Pro and Archer

Printed on acid-free paper. ∞

Printed in the United States of America

10 9 8 7 6 5 4 3 2 1

Contents

Introduction   1

CHAPTER ONE
A Pure Theory of Law?   12

CHAPTER TWO
Social Rules at the Foundations of Law   35

CHAPTER THREE
Authority, Conventions, and the Normativity of Law   60

CHAPTER FOUR
Is Law Determined by Morality?   84

CHAPTER FIVE
Is Legal Philosophy Normative?   109

CHAPTER SIX
The Language of Law   136

Bibliography   161

Index   167

Philosophy of Law

Introduction

IN THE EARLY SUMMER OF 2008, California highways were dot-
ted with electronic signposts displaying the following message:
"Hands Free Phone, July 1st, It's The Law!" California drivers
would have known exactly what the signposts referred to: Earlier
that year, a new law was enacted by the California legislature that
prohibits the use of cellular phones while driving unless using
a hands-free device.[1] The signposts were not, of course, the law.
They just reminded drivers, informed them, as it were, that "it's
the law!" Notice that this is an interesting kind of information,
because it conveys two different types of content: descriptive and
prescriptive. In one sense, the message informs us about something that happened, some *events* that took place in Sacramento
earlier that year. But in a clear second sense, the message reminds
us that we *ought* to behave in a certain way—that is, we are now
obliged to use a hands-free device if we want to use a mobile
phone while driving; after all, it is now *the law*. And of course,
these two kinds of content are causally related: The legal obligation to use a hands-free device somehow follows from the fact
that certain events had actually taken place, namely, that there
were some particular people in Sacramento who gathered in a
certain place, talked, raised their hands, signed a document, and
so forth.

It is in thinking about this duality of content that philosophy
of law emerges. The law is, by and large, a system of norms. Law's
essential character is prescriptive: It purports to guide action,
alter modes of behavior, constrain the practical deliberation of
its subjects; generally speaking, the law purports to give us reasons for action. Needless to say, not all laws impose obligations.

---

[1] California Vehicle Code 2008, section 23123: "(a) A person shall not drive a
motor vehicle while using a wireless telephone unless that telephone is specifically
designed and configured to allow hands-free listening and talking, and is used in
that manner while driving."

A great many laws in a developed legal system grant rights of various kinds, provide legal powers to change other rights and obligations, and establish institutions defining their legal powers and authorities. Nevertheless, in spite of the great diversity of types of norms that law comprises, by and large legal norms are of a prescriptive kind. Laws do not purport to describe aspects of the world; they do not consist of propositions about the way things are. In one way or another, laws purport to affect or modify people's conduct, and mostly by providing them with reasons for action. Let us call this aspect of the law its essential normative character.[2]

The law is a rather unique normative system, however, in that the norms of law are typically products of human creation. Although there may be exceptions, by and large the law is something that is created by deliberate human action. Legal norms are enacted by legislatures or various agencies or are created by judges in rendering their judicial decisions. Law is typically a product of an act of will. If we combine these two observations, we can begin to see the main problem that has preoccupied philosophers of law: how to explain this unique normative significance of events in the world that are, basically, human actions, acts of will, so to speak, performed by groups or individuals? And what does this normative significance consist in?

Legal philosophers have understood this problem to consist of two main questions: One is a question about the very idea of legality, or *legal validity*, and the other is a question about the concept of *legal normativity*. Consider the California signposts again. They tell us that there is something we now ought to do, and that we ought to do it because "it's the law!" The first question, about legal validity, is the question of what makes it the case that this normative content (that you ought to use a hands-free device while driving) is, indeed, the law. And the second question is about the nature of the "ought" that is prescribed by such norms.

---

[2] The law may have other normative aspects that are not directly instantiated by providing reasons for action. The law may set an example or a standard for conduct in various other forms, or it may even purport to influence people's beliefs and attitudes.

Let us begin with the concept of legal validity. When we say that "it is the law that X" or "the law requires you to X," and similar locutions, we implicitly rely on the idea of legal validity. For any given normative content, it may be legally valid in a given jurisdiction at some given time, or not legally valid, or, possibly, it may be in some doubt whether it is legally valid or not. Unlike moral or logical validity, however, the idea of legal validity is closely tied to a place and time. The hands-free mobile phone requirement is now legally valid in California but not in Nevada (where no such legal requirement applies), and it is valid at the moment, but had not been so two years ago. In short, whenever it is suggested that *the law is* such and such, the question of when and where is relevant. Nevertheless, it is widely assumed that some philosophical account should be available to determine what are generally the conditions that make a certain normative content legally valid. What makes it the case, or what are the kinds of factors that determine, that a certain normative content is the law in a given time and place? In other words, the philosophical question about legal validity is this:

> What are the *general conditions* that make any proposition of the form—"X [some normative content] *is the law at time* t *in* C [with respect to a given place and/or population]"—true (or false)?

Note that the generality of this question is of crucial importance. Every lawyer knows what makes the content of, say, the California Vehicle Code legally valid: the fact that the code had been duly enacted by the California legislature according to procedures prescribed by the California Constitution. Philosophers, however, are interested in a much more general aspect of this question: What we seek to understand is, what are, generally, the conditions that constitute the idea of legal validity? Would these conditions consist only in social facts, like actions and events that took place at a certain place and time? If so, what makes those actions, and not others, legally significant? And perhaps the conditions of legal validity are not exhausted by such facts; perhaps there are some further, normative considerations that have to apply as well. Is it the case that the content of the relevant norm

3

also bears on its legal validity, and not just the manner in which it came to be created? Furthermore, there is also the possibility that legal validity is not necessarily tied to actions and events that have somehow created the norm. Some prominent legal philosophers have argued that the legal validity of norms can sometimes be deduced by moral reasoning. A certain normative content can be legally valid because it is content that reasoning, based on moral and other similar considerations, would lead us to conclude is valid under the circumstances. So these are the general questions that arise with respect to the very idea of legality; what we seek to articulate is an account of the general conditions that constitute the legal validity of norms.

Roughly, three main schools of thought have emerged in response to the general questions concerning the conditions of legal validity: According to one school of thought—called *legal positivism*, which emerged during the early nineteenth century[3] and has retained considerable influence ever since—the conditions of legal validity are constituted by social facts. Legality is constituted by a complex set of facts relating to people's actions, beliefs, and attitudes, and those social facts basically exhaust the conditions of legal validity. As we will see in the first two chapters, a very important aspect of the debate here relates to the possibility of reduction: Can the conditions of legal validity be reduced to facts of a non-normative type?

Another school of thought, originating in a much older tradition, called *natural law*, maintains that the conditions of legal validity—though necessarily tied to actions and events that take place—are not exhausted by those law-creating acts/events. The content of the putative norm, mostly its moral content, also bears on its legal validity. Normative content that does not meet a certain minimal threshold of moral acceptability cannot be *legally* valid. As the famous dictum of St. Augustine has it: *lex iniusta non est lex* (unjust law is not law). Whether this view is rightly attributable to the Thomist natural law tradition, as it often has been, is a contentious issue, but one that I will not consider in any

---

[3] Although the basic ideas of nineteenth-century legal positivism are clearly traceable to the political philosophy of Thomas Hobbes.

detail here;[4] and whether it is a view that still has any philosophical support is questionable.

A third view about the conditions of legal validity, which has drawn some inspiration from the natural law tradition but differs from it in essential details, maintains that moral content is not a necessary condition of legality, but it may be a sufficient one. According to this view, moral-political reasoning is sometimes sufficient to conclude that a certain normative content is legally valid, that it forms part of the law in a given context. As we shall see in chapter 4, there are two main versions of this view: one articulated by Ronald Dworkin and another that has emerged as a significant modification of traditional legal positivism.

Neither legal positivism nor its critiques form a unified theory about legal validity. There are important variations and divergent views within each one of these jurisprudential traditions. There is a recurring theme, however, that the debate centers on, and it is about the possibility of detaching the conditions that constitute legal validity from the evaluative content of the putative norms in question. Legal positivism maintains that the conditions of validity are detached from content, while critics of this tradition maintain a nondetachment view. According to the latter views, what the law *is* partly depends on what the law ought to be in some relevant sense of *ought*.

Everybody agrees, or so it seems, that the law purports to provide us with reasons for action. Law's essential normative character is not in any serious doubt. The doubts concern the question of what kind of reasons legal norms provide. Take, for example, the simple notion of a legal obligation—that is, assume that a certain legal norm prescribes that "all persons with feature F ought to ☐ under circumstances C." What exactly is the nature of this "ought"? And how is it related, if at all, to a moral ought?

The crucial first step here is to distinguish between two different kinds of concerns we may have. One concern relates to the question of a moral obligation to obey a legal obligation. The fact that the law purports to impose an obligation to φ does

---

[4] John Finnis famously argued that Thomist natural law is not committed to this thesis. See his *Natural Law and Natural Rights.*

not necessarily entail that there is, therefore, a moral obligation to ☐. Or, put differently, a legal ought is not necessarily an all-things-considered ought. The fact that one has a legal obligation to ☐ leaves it open to question whether one ought to ☐, morally speaking, or all things considered.[5] It is widely recognized, however, that the question of whether there is a moral obligation to comply with a legal obligation is a moral issue, not one that can be determined on grounds pertaining to the nature of law. Although the moral issue may partly depend on how we understand the nature of law and its normative character, ultimately it is a moral question, to be determined on moral grounds, whether there is a general moral obligation to obey the law, and under what circumstances.

The question that legal philosophers are interested in, however, is different: It is the question about what a legal obligation (and other types of legal prescription) consists in. What exactly is the nature of this "ought" that the law purports to impose on its subjects? Is it like a moral obligation, just from a different perspective? Or perhaps a species of moral obligation that would arise under certain conditions? Or perhaps a legal ought is reducible to a predictive statement that, if one does not comply with the legal requirement, one is likely to incur some undesirable consequences?

It is very difficult to subsume the various answers philosophers have offered to these questions about the nature of legal normativity under particular schools of thought. It might be tempting to think that the different schools of thought about the concept of legality would also entail correspondingly different views about the concept of legal normativity. Unfortunately, this is not quite so. There is, however, this general connection: The more you tend to regard legal obligation as a kind of, or on a par with, moral obligation, the more you would be inclined to resist a detachment of legal validity from morality. There is, in other words, some pressure here: If you think about the content of the law as the kind of normative content that provides us with moral reasons for action,

---

[5] I am not suggesting that a moral ought is an all-things-considered ought, or vice versa. These are just two similar ways to think about the question.

you would tend to think of legality itself as conditioned on some moral content. If you allow for the conditions of legality to be detached from the moral content of the law, it becomes difficult to hold the view that the law necessarily, or even typically, provides us with moral reasons for action. To be sure, this is just a pressure, not an entailment relation. Whether there are ways to resist this pressure is something that we will have to see in some detail as we go along.

These two main questions about the nature of law, about the conditions of legal validity and about legal normativity, have recently generated another kind of debate in contemporary philosophy of law, one about the nature of the enterprise itself. If, indeed, the factual aspects of law cannot be detached from its normative content, perhaps a philosophical account of what the law is cannot be detached from the normative content that is ascribed to law. Philosophy of law, according to this nondetachment view, is necessarily a normative type of philosophy—that is, a type of philosophy that necessarily engages in questions about what law ought to be. So here we get to a controversy about the nature of legal philosophy: Is it the kind of theory that purports only to describe something, telling us what it is, or is it the kind of philosophy that necessarily incorporates some views about the way things ought to be? This methodological debate about the nature of legal philosophy has become one of the central themes in contemporary philosophy of law. Not surprisingly, those who hold a nondetachment view about the relations between law's factual and normative aspects also tend to hold a nondetachment view about legal philosophy's descriptive and evaluative components. Whether these two types of nondetachment views are necessarily linked and, if so, how precisely they are linked, is a difficult question that will be addressed at different parts of the book.

These two main themes, namely, the relations between the factual and the normative and between substance and method, will inform the main argument of this book. I will try to show that the debates about the possibility of detachment in both substance and method, and the subtle relations between them, have informed a great deal of the theorizing in legal philosophy during the last century. And I will try to show that a substantial part of these debates centers on the question of the possibility of reduction.

In chapter 1, I will discuss Hans Kelsen's influential attempt to present a "pure" theory of law, and the reasons for its failure. I will try to show that Kelsen's pure theory of law is the most striking—and in many ways, still the most interesting—defense of a complete detachment view, both in method and substance. The main reason for the failure of this project, I will argue, is that it identified the detachment view with antireductionism. Kelsen thought that a theory about the nature of law should avoid any reduction of legal facts to facts of any other type, either social or moral.

In chapter 2, I will present some of H.L.A. Hart's main contributions to legal philosophy. Hart's *The Concept of Law* is widely regarded as the single most important contribution to legal philosophy in the twentieth century. Indeed, I will try to show that Hart's theory is the most consistent and sustained attempt to develop a detachment view of law and legal philosophy, and one that is thoroughly reductive. But here I will introduce another separation, or detachment, that Hart's theory attempted, and one that I think is less successful: the detachment of law from state sovereignty. The legal positivist tradition, from Hobbes to the main positivists of the nineteenth century, conceived of law as the instrument of political sovereignty, largely influenced by the emergence of the modern state. Law, according to this view, consists of the commands of the political sovereign. Hart was at pains to show that this identification of law with state sovereignty is profoundly misguided; law is independently grounded on social rules, not on political sovereignty. In fact, Hart argued that traditional legal positivism got the direction wrong here: Law does not emanate from political sovereignty because our concept of political sovereignty is partly dependent on legal norms. I will argue that Hart's attempt to separate our understanding of law from the concept of sovereignty is only partly successful. He is right that we need to avoid forging too tight a connection between law and state, but, as Joseph Raz has shown, it is equally important to realize that there is an essential connection between law and authority. An analysis of the essentially authoritative nature of law, and an attempt to reconcile it with Hart's conception of law as based on social rules, forms the topic of chapter 3. In this chapter I will bring together some of Hart's main insights about the nature of law with those of Raz, arguing that a conventionalist account of law's foundations can accommodate the best insights of both, at least with certain modifications.

In chapter 4, I will consider the contemporary versions of the *substantive* nondetachment view about the nature of law. As noted earlier, this view takes two main forms: According to Dworkin's influential theory, law's content can never be detached from normative considerations. What the law is—always, and necessarily—depends on certain evaluative considerations about what it ought to be. A more moderate version of this nondetachment view holds that whether the content of law can or cannot be detached from normative considerations is a contingent matter, depending on the norms that happen to prevail in a given legal system, and thus the nondetachment view is at least sometimes true. The main argument of this chapter will be that both of these views are mistaken. The argument here will be completed, however, only in the last chapter. Before that, in chapter 5, I consider the *methodological* variant of the nondetachment view. According to this variant, any philosophical theory about the nature of law, including legal positivism, necessarily implicates some normative views about what the law ought to be. There are several versions of this claim, and I will distinguish among them, arguing that some versions of this type of nondetachment thesis are actually not at odds with the descriptive aspirations of Hart's legal philosophy, while those that are, fail on their merits. Properly understood, Hart's methodological detachment view is defensible.

Chapter 6 focuses on the role of language and interpretation in understanding the content of the law. The argument here is motivated by Dworkin's argument that we can never grasp what the law says without interpretation. Since, as he argues, interpretation is partly, but necessarily, an evaluative matter, understanding what the law requires is necessarily dependent on some evaluative considerations. I will argue in this chapter that this conception of what it takes to understand a legal directive is based on a misunderstanding of language and linguistic communication. An attempt to clarify some of the semantic and pragmatic aspects of what the law says forms the main objective of this chapter. One purpose is to show that when linguistic considerations are taken into account in the appropriate ways, we will realize that interpretation becomes the exception, not the standard form of understanding what the law says. Another purpose of this chapter is to show how certain pragmatic aspects of understanding a speech situation can be used to clarify the distinction between understanding what the law says and interpreting it. This last chapter, then, completes a defense of a fairly strong detachment view about the nature of law, both in method and substance.

Legal philosophy is not confined to the kinds of issues that are discussed in this book. A great deal of philosophical work is brought to bear on particular legal domains, such as torts, contracts, criminal responsibility and state punishment, statutory and constitutional interpretation, and many others. This book is focused on the philosophical controversies that concern the general nature of law. Philosophy of tort law and of contracts, and such, each deserves a book-length introduction of its own. Furthermore, it would be presumptuous to claim that a philosophical understanding of the nature of law must be a prologue to any philosophical inquiry into the nature of particular legal domains. Many issues that interest philosophers in such domains as criminal law, or torts, or contracts are mostly moral issues about the underlying justifications of particular legal doctrines. As such, they do not really depend on any particular understanding of the general nature of law. The question of whether legal validity can be reduced to social facts or not, which will be discussed in this book at some length, has simply no bearing on the question of how best to account for the various notions of responsibility deployed in criminal law, or on the question of whether the main doctrines of tort law are best understood in terms of corrective justice. These lines of inquiry are quite independent of one another.

There are, however, several philosophical interests in law that do depend, albeit sometimes indirectly, on general jurisprudence and the kinds of questions discussed in this book. As we will see in chapters 4 and 6, some of the main questions about the nature of statutory interpretation are closely entangled with the main questions about the nature of law and how best to account for it.

The rule of law—and its virtues—is yet another issue, widely discussed in the literature, that also depends on some of the general philosophical views about the nature of law. Most writers on the rule of law—philosophers, lawyers, and political scientists—assume that there is something special about *rule by law* that makes it a desirable form of governance. Thus their assumption has to be that legalism, per se, is good in some respect and worthy of appreciation. But of course, any such view must be based on some conception of what legalism is—which is to say that it must depend, at least to some extent, on what law, in general, is, and what makes it a special instrument of social control.

This book is focused on some of the main issues that have preoccupied philosophy about the nature of law in the last century and a half or so. The book is not meant to be comprehensive, even in its limited focus, and it certainly does not cover most of the issues that philosophers interested in law work on. The book is not written as a report but as an argument for a particular position. Many of my colleagues would disagree with the position. Philosophy, however, aims at truth, not consensus. A fruitful disagreement is the best one can hope for.

I am greatly indebted to friends and colleagues who have commented on drafts of the manuscript. Scott Soames and Gideon Yaffe were kind enough to read it all and provide me with invaluable comments and suggestions. Joseph Raz has been extremely helpful by commenting on several chapters. Thanks also go to Chaim Gans, Mark Schroeder, Stephen Finlay, and the reviewers of Princeton University Press for comments and constructive suggestions.

A Pure Theory of Law?

IN PHILOSOPHY, as in other disciplines, we often try to explain one kind of things in terms of another. Generally, this is what a theoretical explanation amounts to. If we manage to provide an explanation of a certain aspect of the world that seems problematic, in terms of some other aspect that is less problematic, we will have certainly made some progress. Some types of explanation, in philosophy as well as in science, have the unique character we call *reductive*: If there is a clear demarcation of one type of discourse or class of statements, and we can provide a full explanation of that class of statements in terms of some other type or class, then the explanation is reductive. For example, if we could fully explain the realm of our mental life in terms of truths about the physical aspects of the world, we would have provided a reductive explanation of the mental to the physical realm. In some cases, however, philosophical explanation goes in the opposite direction, striving to show why a reduction of one kind of phenomenon to another, or of one kind of explanation to another, is impossible. It is with this latter, antireductionist theory of law that I want to begin here.[1]

---

[1] Different conceptions of what would count as a reductive explanation may be relevant to different domains. One type of reduction, which is sometimes called *semantic*, would have to satisfy the condition that the basic vocabulary of a theory, say T1, could be fully expressed by the axioms and vocabulary of a different theory, T2. If this condition is met, then we have a full semantic reduction of T1 to T2. Very few legal theorists have thought about reduction in this semantic sense (with the exception, perhaps, of John Austin, discussed in the next chapter). The type of reduction more relevant to legal theory is *constitutive* or *metaphysical*: The idea of a metaphysical reduction is to show that a distinct type of phenomenon is actually constituted and fully explicable by a different, more foundational, type of phenomenon or set of facts. Philosophers also discuss a third type of reduction,

The clearest and most articulate attempt to provide an antire-ductionist theory of law was made by Hans Kelsen, in the first half of the twentieth century. Kelsen characterized his aspiration as an attempt to present *a pure theory* of law.[2] In his own words, the as-piration was "to develop . . . a legal theory purified of all political ideology and every element of the natural sciences, a theory con-scious, so to speak, of the autonomy of the object of its enquiry and thereby conscious of its own unique character."[3]

It is no accident that law is flanked here by ideology (or, we should rather say, morality) on one side, and natural science on the other. The temptation to ground law on moral-ideological foundations stems from its essential normative character. Law is not a theoretical domain; it is there to make a practical differ-ence. The law purports to give us reasons for action. It is, there-fore, inevitable that we ask ourselves why the fact that an action is required by law would count in favor of doing it. It is natu-ral to assume that a legal requirement can constitute a fact that would count in favor of doing something only if law is good, at least in some respect. Now, of course, not all law is really good, morally or otherwise. But there is this strong temptation to sug-gest that what the law *is*, or what would count as a legal require-ment, somehow depends on what is good (or right, or morally re-quired). If nothing else, it would make it easier to explain why the fact that the law requires something counts in favor of doing it. But this temptation, Kelsen argued, is precisely the one that needs

---

or quasi-reduction, called supervenience: A realm X would supervene on realm Y if and only if there are no changes or modifications observable in Y without cor-responding observable changes or modifications in X. The question of whether supervenience is a genuine reductive relation or not is debated in the literature. I will largely ignore these complicated issues here.

[2] Kelsen's most important books on the pure theory of law are the first edition of his *Reine Rechtslehre*, published in 1934, and recently translated to English under the title *Introduction to the Problems of Legal Theory*, and the second edition (con-siderably extended), which Kelsen published in 1960, *Pure Theory of Law*. These books are abbreviated here as PT1 and PT2 respectively. In addition, most of the themes in these two books also appear in Kelsen's *General Theory of Law and State*, abbreviated here as GT.

[3] Kelsen's preface, PT1. Antireductionism is only one core aspect of Kelsen's idea about the purity of a theory of law. It is the only aspect that interests me here.

to be resisted. Philosophy of law, he thought, should be confined to an explanation of what law is. Whether the law in general, or any particular law, is good or bad, is a separate question—one for moral philosophers to figure out. In other words, Kelsen assumed in advance, as it were, that if a detachment view of legality, one that makes legal validity completely detached from the moral content of the law, can be provided, it would be a better kind of explanation of the nature of law.[4]

But now think about the route that we are led to: If we are to explain what the law is—in particular, what the general conditions of legal validity are—in terms that make no allusion to the moral or other normative content of legal norms, we would have to show that there are certain facts, non-normative facts, that determine what counts as law. Let us say that there are some social facts about people's actions, beliefs, and attitudes that fully determine what counts as law. If such an explanation is available, have we not provided a reduction of law to social facts? Have we not just explained one kind of thing in terms of another kind? Moreover, if the explanation of legality is provided in terms of social facts, can we resist the conclusion that it is better if sociology takes over? Why not, then, strive to reduce legal theory to some other kind of theory, one that may be better equipped to explain social phenomena? So this is the opposite temptation that Kelsen was at pains to resist, the temptation to reduce legal theory to sociology, or any other kind of a "natural science."

Thus, the main challenge for a theory of law, as Kelsen saw it, is to provide an explanation of legality and legal normativity without an attempt to reduce jurisprudence, or "legal science," to other domains. In this antireductionist aspiration, I think that Kelsen was not entirely successful. His theory actually invites a certain type of reduction of legal validity to social facts, a reduction that Kelsen has strikingly refused to admit. In this chapter I will argue that, at least in this crucial respect, Kelsen's antireductionism fails, and that there is an important lesson to learn from this failure. In another sense, however, concerning the general

---

[4] This, of course, is one of the main reasons why Kelsen is rightly seen as a legal positivist.

reducibility of legal philosophy to sociology, Kelsen's antireductionism is sound, and there is an important lesson to be learned from that too.

THE BASIC NORM

You may recall that in the state of California, it is now legally forbidden to use a mobile phone while driving unless using a hands-free device. But why is that really the case? It had not been the case just two years earlier; what is it that changed since? Here is what happened: In December 2007, a group of about 120 people gathered in Sacramento, in the state capitol building; argued about this issue; eventually raised their hands in an answer to the question of whether they approved a certain document; and then transferred the document to be signed by a person called Arnold Schwarzenegger, which he promptly did. Kelsen was quite right to note that these kinds of actions and events that I just described are not the law. To say that what I described is the *enactment* of a new law is to *interpret* these actions and events in a certain way:

> What makes such an event a legal act is its meaning, the objective sense that attaches to the act. The specifically legal sense of the event in question, its own peculiarly legal meaning, comes by way of a norm whose content refers to the event and confers legal meaning on it; the act can be interpreted, then, according to this norm. The norm functions as a scheme of interpretation.[5]

The law, Kelsen claims, is a scheme of interpretation. Its reality, or objectivity, if you like, resides in the sphere of meaning; we attach a legal-normative meaning to certain actions and events. But then, of course, the question is why certain acts or events have such a legal meaning and others do not. To put matters very simply, think about it this way: What exactly is it that explains the fact that if I proclaim that "everybody ought to avoid using mobile phones while driving," it is a legally meaningless statement?

But when the California legislature enacts a norm with the same content, it is the law in California that drivers ought to avoid using mobile phones while driving. Surely, there is nothing in the content of this speech act—which is identical in both cases—that would explain the difference. So what is the relevant difference? Kelsen's answer to this question is surprisingly simple: An act or an event gains its legal-normative meaning by another legal norm that confers this normative meaning on it. An act can create or modify the law if it instantiates another, "higher" legal norm that authorizes its creation in that way. And the "higher" legal norm, in turn, is legally valid if and only if it has been created in accord with yet another, "higher" norm that authorizes its enactment in that way. In other words, it is *the law* in the United States that the California legislature can enact traffic regulations, and that my proclamations—wise and commendable as they may be—are legally meaningless. But what makes this the law? The California Constitution confers this power on the state legislature to enact laws within certain prescribed boundaries of content and jurisdiction. But what makes the California Constitution legally valid? The answer is that the legal validity of the Constitution of California derives from an authorization granted by the U.S. Constitution. What makes the U.S. constitution legally valid? Surely, not the fact that the U.S. Constitution proclaims itself to be "the supreme law of the land." Any document can say that, but only the particular document of the U.S. Constitution is actually the supreme law in the United States.

The problem is that here the chain of authorization comes to an end. There is no higher legal norm that authorizes the enactment of the (original) U.S. Constitution. At this point, Kelsen famously argued, one must *presuppose* the legal validity of the Constitution. At some stage, in every legal system, we get to an authorizing norm that has not been authorized by any other legal norm, and thus it has to be presupposed to be legally valid. The normative content of this presupposition is what Kelsen has called the *basic norm*. The basic norm is the content of the presupposition of the legal validity of the (first, historical) constitution of the relevant legal system.[6]

[6] See, e.g., GT, 110–11.

As Kelsen saw it, there is simply no alternative. More precisely, any alternative would violate David Hume's injunction against deriving an "ought" from an "is." Hume famously argued that any practical argument that concludes with some prescriptive statement, a statement of the kind that one ought to do this or that, would have to contain at least one prescriptive statement in its premises. If *all* the premises of an argument are descriptive, telling us that this or that *is* the case, then there is no prescriptive conclusion that can logically follow. Kelsen took this argument very seriously. He observed that the actions and events that constitute, say, the enactment of a law, are all within the sphere of what "is" the case—they are all within the sphere of actions and events that take place in the world. Legal norms, the law, are within the sphere of "ought" statements—they are norms that purport to guide conduct. Thus, to get an "ought" type of conclusion from a set of "is" premises, one must point to some "ought" premise in the background—an "ought" that confers the normative meaning on the relevant type of "is." Since the actual, legal, chain of validity comes to an end, we inevitably reach a point where the "ought" has to be presupposed, and this is the presupposition of the basic norm.

Now you might think that this is a rather superficial understanding of Hume, or perhaps it just takes Hume's argument too seriously.[7] I will come to agree with that, but first we need a more complete picture of Kelsen's views. The idea of the basic norm serves three theoretical functions in Kelsen's theory of law. The first is to ground a nonreductive explanation of legal validity. The second function is to ground a nonreductive explanation of the normativity of law. The third function is to explain the systematic nature of legal norms. Since I want to focus mostly on the first two explanatory functions, let me just say a few words on the third one. These three issues are not unrelated.

Kelsen rightly noticed that legal norms necessarily come in systems. There are no free-floating legal norms. If you tell me that

---

[7] Whether Hume's "is/ought" fallacy is really a fallacy is philosophically contentious. Some contemporary philosophers doubt that "ought" cannot be derived from "is." My argument in this chapter does not take a stance on this question. I will assume, *arguendo*, that Hume is right and "ought" cannot be derived from "is," but nothing in my own views here really depends on the truth of this.

the law requires a will to be attested by two witnesses, I should ask you which legal system you are talking about. Is it Canadian law, German law, or the law in some other legal system? Furthermore, legal systems are themselves organized in a hierarchical structure, manifesting a great deal of complexity but also a certain systematic unity. We talk about Canadian law, or German law, and the like, not only because these are separate countries in which there is law. They are also separate legal systems, manifesting a certain cohesion and unity. This systematic unity Kelsen meant to capture by the following two postulates:

(1) Every two norms that derive their validity from one basic norm belong to the same legal system.
(2) All legal norms of a given legal system derive their validity from one basic norm.

Whether these two postulates are actually true is a contentious issue. Joseph Raz argued that they are both inaccurate, at best.[8] Two legal norms can derive their validity from the same basic norm but fail to belong to the same system as, for example, in the case of an orderly secession whereby a new legal system is created by the legal authorization of another. Nor is it necessarily true that all the legally valid norms of a given system derive their validity from the same basic norm.[9]

Be this as it may, even if Kelsen erred about the details of the unity of legal systems,[10] his main insight remains true, and quite important. It is true that law is essentially systematic, and it is also

[8] Raz, *The Authority of Law*, 127–29.

[9] A good example of this can be given from the present situation in the European Union countries: Some of the norms that are legally valid in the European Union countries derive their validity from the European Community treaties and legislation, while others derive their validity from the basic norm of the municipal legal system. Still, we would not be inclined to say that in each and every EU country two separate legal systems are in force. In short, Kelsen's assumption that legal systems necessarily have a neat hierarchical structure that can be subsumed under one basic norm seems to be false, as a matter of fact.

[10] Kelsen may have also conflated two issues here: legal validity and membership in a legal system. He seems to have assumed that these two criteria are necessarily equivalent. But that is not the case. A given norm can be legally valid in one system, at least for certain purposes or in a given context, even if the norm belongs

true that the idea of legal validity and law's systematic nature are very closely linked. In fact, we encountered an aspect of this connection between legal validity and the systematic nature of law when we noted (in the introduction) that legal validity is necessarily spatiotemporal. Norms are legally valid within a given system; they have to form part of a system of norms that is in force in a given place and time.[11]

This last point brings us to another observation that is central to Kelsen's theory about the relations between legal validity and, what he called, "efficacy." The latter is a term of art in Kelsen's writings: A norm is *efficacious* if it is actually (generally) followed by the relevant population. Thus, "a norm is considered to be legally valid," Kelsen wrote, "on the condition that it belongs to a system of norms, to an order which, on the whole, is efficacious."[12] So the relationship is this: Efficacy is not a condition of legal validity of individual norms. Any given norm can be legally valid even if nobody follows it. (For example, think about a new law, just enacted; it is legally valid even if nobody has yet had an opportunity to comply with it.) However, a norm can only be legally valid if it belongs to a system, a legal order that is by and large actually practiced by a certain population. And thus the idea of legal validity, as Kelsen admits, is closely tied to this reality of a social practice; a legal system exists, as it were, only as a social reality—a reality that consists in the fact that people actually follow certain norms.

What about the basic norm? Is efficacy a condition of its validity? One might have thought that Kelsen would have opted for a negative answer. After all, the basic norm is a presupposition that is logically required to render the validity of law intelligible. This would seem to be the whole point of an antireductionist explanation of legal validity: Since we cannot derive an "ought" from an "is," some "ought" must be presupposed in the background that

---

to another legal system. A contract, for example, that is under the jurisdiction of English law may be governed by norms that belong to French contract law.

[11] Admittedly, this is somewhat rough; the jurisdiction a law claims is not necessarily identical to the jurisdiction it actually has (de facto), and the jurisdiction law sometimes claims is extraterritorial. Complications abound here, but the general spatiotemporal aspect of legal validity is an essential aspect of law.

[12] GT, 42.

would enable us to interpret certain acts or events as having legal significance. Kelsen, however, quite explicitly admits that efficacy *is* a condition of the validity of the basic norm: A basic norm is legally valid if and only if it is actually followed in a given population. In fact, as I will try to explain in a moment, Kelsen had no choice here. And this is precisely why at least one crucial aspect of his antireductionism is bound to fail. Let me explain this in some detail.

RELATIVISM AND REDUCTION

Common wisdom has it that Kelsen's argument for the presupposition of the basic norm takes the form of a Kantian transcendental argument.[13] The structure is as follows:

(1) P *is possible* only if Q
(2) P is possible (or, possibly P)
(3) Therefore, Q

In Kelsen's argument, P stands for the fact that legal norms are "ought" statements,[14] and Q is the presupposition of the basic norm. In other words, the necessary presupposition of the basic norm is derived from the possibility conditions for ascribing legal significance to actions and events. In order to interpret an action as one of creating or modifying the law, it is necessary to show that the relevant legal significance of the act/event is conferred on it by some other legal norm. At some point, as previously noted, we necessarily run out of legal norms that confer the relevant validity on law-creating acts, and at that point the legal validity

---

[13] See Paulson's introduction to PT1. I think that Kelsen gradually changed his mind about the question of whether he espoused a transcendental argument. In his earlier writings, he probably thought that he did, but by the time of the publication of GT, in the mid-1940s, he seemed to have discarded this Kantian version of his argument. In any case, my point in the text is that the Kantian version makes no sense in the overall context of his argument.

[14] Kelsen denied that "ought" statements are propositions; he thought that such expressions were not truth-apt. I will largely ignore this aspect of Kelsen's theory; it does not affect my argument.

has to be presupposed. The content of this presupposition is the basic norm.

I think that it would be a mistake to look for an explanation of Kelsen's argument in the logic of Kant's transcendental argument. First, Kant employed a transcendental argument to establish the necessary presuppositions of some categories and modes of perception that are essential for rational cognition, or so he thought. They form deep, universal, and necessary features of human cognition. Suffice it to recall that it was Hume's skepticism about knowledge that Kant strove to answer by his transcendental argument. Kelsen, however, remains much closer to Hume's skeptical views than to Kant's rationalism. In particular, Kelsen was very skeptical of any objective grounding of morality, Kant's moral theory included. Kelsen's view of morality was relativist all the way down. (More on this below.) Second, and not unrelated, as we shall see, Kelsen explicitly rejected the idea that the basic norm (in law, or of any other normative domain) is something like a necessary feature or category of human cognition. The presupposition of a basic norm is optional. One does not have to accept the normativity of law; anarchism, as a rejection of law's normative validity, is certainly an option, Kelsen maintained. The basic norm is presupposed only by those who accept the "ought"—that is, the normative validity, of the law. But one is not rationally compelled to have this attitude:

> The Pure Theory describes the positive law as an objectively valid order and states that this interpretation is possible only under the condition that a basic norm is presupposed. . . . The Pure Theory thereby characterizes this interpretation as possible, not necessary, and presents the objective validity of positive law only as conditional—namely conditioned by the presupposed basic norm.[15]

A comparison to religion, that Kelsen himself offered, might be helpful here. The normative structure of religious beliefs is very similar, he maintained, to that of legal normativity. It has the same logic: Religious beliefs about what one ought to do

---

[15] PT2, 217–18.

ultimately derive from one's beliefs about God's commands. God's commands, however, would only have normative validity for those who presuppose the basic norm of their respective religion—that one ought to obey God's commands. Thus the normativity of religion, like that of the law, rests on the presupposition of its basic norm. But in both cases, as, in fact, with any other normative system, the presupposition of the basic norm is logically required only of those who regard the relevant norms as reasons for their actions. Thus, whether you actually presuppose the relevant basic norm is a matter of choice; it is an ideological option, as it were, not something that is dictated by Reason. Similarly, the normativity of law, presupposed by its basic norm, is optional: "An anarchist, for instance, who denied the validity of the hypothetical basic norm of positive law . . . will view its positive regulation of human relationships . . . as mere power relations."[16]

Relativism, as always, comes with a price. We have not yet said anything about the question of what it is that determines the content of the basic norm. What is the content of the basic norm that one needs to presuppose in order to render positive law intelligible as a normative legal order? The simple answer is that what one presupposes here is precisely the normative validity of *positive law*—the law that is practiced by a certain population. The validity of the basic norm, as noted briefly earlier, is conditional on its "efficacy." The content of the basic norm of any given legal system is determined by the actual practices that prevail in the relevant community. As Kelsen himself repeatedly argued, a successful revolution brings about a radical change in the content of the basic norm. Suppose, for example, that in a given legal system the basic norm is that the constitution enacted by Rex One is binding. At a certain point, a coup d'état takes place and a republican government is successfully installed. At this point, Kelsen admitted, "one presupposes a new basic norm, no longer the basic norm delegating law making authority to the monarch, but a basic norm delegating authority to the revolutionary government."[17]

[16] GT, 413.
[17] PT1, 59.

Did Kelsen violate his own adherence to Hume's injunction against deriving "ought" from an "is" here? One gets the clear impression that Kelsen was aware of a serious difficulty in his position. In both editions of the *Pure Theory of Law*, Kelsen toyed with the idea that perhaps changes in the basic norms of municipal legal systems legally derive from the basic norm of public international law. But this led him to the rather uncomfortable conclusion that there is only one basic norm in the entire world—the basic norm of public international law.[18] Be this as it may, the main worry lies elsewhere. The worry stems from the fact that it is very difficult, if not impossible, to maintain both a profound relativist and an antireductionist position with respect to a given normative domain. If you hold the view that the validity of a type of norm is entirely relative to a certain vantage point—in other words, if what is involved here is only the actual conduct, beliefs/presuppositions, and attitudes of people—it becomes very difficult to detach the explanation of that normativity from the facts that constitute the relevant point of view (the facts about people's actions, beliefs, attitudes, and such). This is what was meant earlier by the comment that Kelsen had no option but to admit that the validity of the basic norm is conditional on its efficacy. The normative relativism that is inherent in Kelsen's conception forces him to ground the content of the basic norm in the social

---

[18] In the first edition of the *Pure Theory of Law* (61–62), Kelsen argued that it follows from the basic norm of international law that state sovereignty is determined by successful control over a given territory. Therefore, the changes in the basic norm that stem from successful revolutions can be accounted for in legalistic terms, relying on the dogmas of international law. The price Kelsen had to pay for this solution, however, was rather high: He was compelled to claim that all municipal legal systems derive their legal validity from international law, and this entails that there is only one basic norm in the entire world—the basic norm of public international law. Although this solution is repeated in the second edition of the *Pure Theory of Law* (214–15), Kelsen presented it there with much more hesitation, perhaps just as an option that would make sense. It is not quite clear that he was willing to adhere to this solution. The hesitation is understandable; after all, the idea that all municipal legal systems derive their legal validity from international law would strike most jurists and legal historians as rather fanciful and anachronistic. And then, the idea that there is only one basic norm in the world, the basic norm of public international law, would seem to be just as incredible.

facts that constitute its content—the facts about actions, beliefs, and attitudes entertained by the population in question. And this makes it very questionable that reductionism can be avoided. In fact, what Kelsen really offered us here is an invitation to provide a reductive explanation of the concept of legal validity in terms of some set of social facts—the facts that constitute the content of any given basic norm.

One might object to this conclusion; surely not every form of normative relativism entails a reductive explanation. That is correct; not every form of relativism entails reductionism. For example, one can hold a nonreductive view about moral reasons for action yet allow for a certain level of relativism about such reasons. One may allow, for instance, that some moral reasons for action are relative to some contingent conditions (for example, reasons to care about friendship are contingent on our psychological makeup and some social realities), or some epistemic constraints (for example, that one may not have a reason to do something if one is in no position to comprehend the reason or the facts that constitute it) or any number of such factors. But in order to avoid reductionism, one would have to keep the relativity of reasons to contingent circumstances somewhat limited and, crucially, explicable by those elements of the theory that are not relative to contingent facts. If all the elements of a normative explanation are relative to some constitutive facts, then those facts provide you with all the explanation you need. In other words, a position that is relativist all the way down is, ipso facto, reductionist as well.[19]

Let me clarify something: Kelsen's problem here is not due to the fact that he was a relativist with respect to every normative system, such as morality, religion, and such; it is not the scope of his relativism that is relevant to the question of reduction. The problem stems from the fact that Kelsen was right about the law. Legal validity *is* essentially relative to the social facts that

[19] I am not suggesting that it goes the other way around. I think that Mark Schroeder gives us a very good reason to resist this view; in identifying a type of normative explanation that he calls constitutive reductionism, he exemplifies that not every type of reductive explanation of normativity is necessarily relativist. Schroeder does not say this, but I think it may well follow from his thesis. See his "Cudworth and Normative Explanations."

constitute the content of the basic norm in each and every legal order. As noted from the outset, legal validity is always relative to a time and place. And now we can see why: because legal validity is determined by the content of the basic norm that is actually followed in a given society. The laws in the United Kingdom, for example, are different from those in the United States because people (mostly judges and other officials) *actually follow* different rules, or basic norms, about what counts as law in their respective jurisdictions. Once Kelsen admits, as he does, that the content of a basic norm is fully determined by practice, it becomes very difficult to understand how the explication of legal validity he offers is nonreductive.

At this point it may be time to revert to the distinction between the concepts of legal validity and legal normativity. Although Kelsen's basic norm purported to explicate both concepts, it is quite possible that we get different results from Kelsen's theory about these two different ideas. My argument so far purports to show that in providing an explanation of the idea of legal validity, Kelsen's theory had not managed to avoid a reductive explanation. The norms that are legally valid in any given legal order are those that derive from its basic norm, but the content of the basic norm is fully determined by social practice. Therefore, the conditions that determine the legal validity of norms turn out, on Kelsen's own account, to consist in facts about people's actions, beliefs, and attitudes—facts that constitute what the basic norm of any given legal system is. But this would seem to have no immediate bearing on how to understand the normativity of law. And Kelsen's views about the normativity of law turn out to be quite interesting.

The first and crucial point to realize is that for Kelsen the idea of normativity is tantamount to a genuine "ought," as it were; it is a justified demand on practical deliberation. A certain content is regarded as normative by an agent if and only if the agent regards that content as *a valid reason for action.* Joseph Raz was right to notice that Kelsen basically agreed with the natural law tradition in this respect; both assume that the normativity of law can only be explained as one would explain the normativity of morality, or religion for that matter, in terms of valid reasons for action.[20] But then, the problem for Kelsen was how to explain the difference between the normativity of law and that of morality; if a legal "ought" is a genuine "ought," what makes a legal obligation distinct from a moral one?[21] Kelsen's answer was that the relevant "ought" is always relative to a given point of view. Each and every type of "ought"—be it religious, moral, or legal—must presuppose a certain point of view, a point of view that is constituted by the basic norm of the relevant normative system.

In other words, Kelsen's conception of legal normativity turns out to be a form of natural law completely relativized to a certain point of view. However, in Kelsen's theory the relevant point of view is distinctly a legal one, not some general conception of morality or Reason. That these two basic norms, or points of view, can come apart is nicely demonstrated by Kelsen's comment that "even an anarchist, if he were a professor of law, could describe positive law as a system of valid norms, without having to approve of this law."[22] The anarchist does not endorse the legal point of view as one that reflects her own moral views about what is right and wrong. Anarchism is understood here as a rejection of the normative validity of law. However, even the anarchist can make an argument about what the law in this or that context requires, and when she makes such an argument, she must presuppose the legal point of view—she must argue *as if* she endorses the basic norm of the relevant legal system. Joseph Raz has called these kinds of statements "detached normative statements"; the anarchist argues *as if* she endorses the basic norm, without actually endorsing it. Another example that Raz gave is this: Suppose that a Catholic priest is an expert in Jewish law; the priest can make various arguments about what Jewish law really requires in this or that context. In such a case, the priest must argue as if he endorses the basic norm of Jewish law, but, of course, being a Catholic, he does not really endorse it. It does not reflect his own views about what is right and wrong.[23]

[20] Raz, *The Authority of Law*, 134–37.
[21] Kelsen was acutely aware of this question; he thought that confusing a legal obligation with a moral one was the main flaw in the natural law tradition.
[22] PT2, 218n.
[23] See Raz, *The Authority of Law*, 153–57.

Here is what emerges so far: The concept of normativity, the sense in which normative content is related to reasons for action, is the same across all these domains. To regard something as normative is to regard it as justified, as a warranted requirement on practical deliberation. However, the difference resides in the difference in points of view. Each basic norm determines a certain point of view. So it turns out that normativity (contra Kant) always consists of *conditional* imperatives: If, and only if, one endorses a certain normative point of view, determined by its basic norm, then the norms that follow from it are reason-giving, so to speak. This enabled Kelsen to maintain the same understanding of the nature of normativity as natural law's conception—normativity qua reasons for action, without having to conflate the normativity of morality with that of law. In other words, the difference between legal normativity and, say, moral normativity is not a difference in normativity (about the nature of normativity, per se) but only in the relevant vantage point that is determined by their different basic norms. What makes legal normativity unique is the uniqueness of its point of view—the legal point of view.

We can set aside the difficulties that such a view raises with respect to morality. Obviously, many philosophers would reject Kelsen's view that moral reasons for action only apply to those who choose to endorse morality's basic norm (whatever it may be). Even if Kelsen was quite wrong about this conditional nature of moral imperatives, he may have been right about the law. However, the question we need to press is whether Kelsen succeeded in providing a nonreductive explanation of legal normativity given the fact that his account of legal validity turned out to be reductive after all.

I think that what got Kelsen in trouble here was not simply the relativity to a point of view; the trouble resided in Kelsen's failure to ground *the choice* of the relevant point of view in anything like Reason or reasons of any kind. By deliberately avoiding any explanation of what it is that might ground an agent's choice of endorsing the legal point of view or any given basic norm, Kelsen left the most pressing questions about the normativity of law unanswered. He gave us no explanation of what makes the presupposition of the legal point of view rational or what makes   27

it rational to regard the requirements of law as binding requirements, as things people ought to do.[24]

Let me try to sum this up. My argument so far aimed to establish that Kelsen's theory of what legal validity consists in, contrary
to his own aspiration, is actually a reductive one. It invites a reductive explanation of legal validity to social facts—facts about
people's conduct, beliefs, and attitudes—that ground the content
of the relevant basic norm. I have also tried to show that there
is something misguided about Kelsen's explanation of the normativity of law. Kelsen was right to assume that normativity can
only be understood in terms of reasons for action; but when the
question arises as to what kind of reasons these are, and what
makes them reasons, Kelsen just invites us to stop asking. These
two points, taken together, imply that we have not yet answered
the main challenge we started with: The challenge, expressed in
terms we have used here, is how to reconcile an explanation of
legal validity, which is, most plausibly, a reductive one, with an
explication of legal normativity, which must be given in terms
of valid reasons for action. Kelsen's answer, that legal obligations
depend on a presupposition that one can either choose to endorse or not, without any explanation of what would ground such
choices and render them rational, remains utterly incomplete. In
chapter 3, we will see how some of Kelsen's views can be amended
and the explanation completed. For the rest of this chapter, however, I will consider a different aspect of Kelsen's antireductionist
aspirations, concerning the nature of legal philosophy itself.

Two Kinds of Reduction

The fact that Kelsen's antireductionism about legal validity is not
convincing does not mean that his antireductionism fails across
the board. We should make a distinction between a theory that offers a reductive explanation of some object of inquiry and a view

---

[24] In chapter 2 we will see that Kelsen had a rather peculiar view about the
individuation of legal norms, maintaining that all legal norms are ultimately addressed to officials.

that strives to reduce one type of theory to another type of theory. Kelsen's pure theory of law strove to avoid both. If my argument is correct, then he failed on the former, but this does not necessarily mean that he was wrong about the latter. The fact that one offers a reductive explanation of what legal validity consists in does not commit one to the view that a theory about the nature of law can be reduced to some other type of theory. In rejecting this latter type of reduction, Kelsen was quite right, or so I shall argue.

Kelsen argued in several places that an overall reduction of jurisprudence to sociology would make no sense. If one is to offer a reduction of jurisprudence to some form of a "natural science," be it sociology or whatever one deems as foundational, "what is certain is that from this viewpoint, the specific meaning of the law is completely lost . . . sociology can define the phenomenon of law, the positive law of a particular community, only by having recourse to the concept of law as defined by normative jurisprudence. Sociological jurisprudence presupposes this concept."[25]

Remember that according to Kelsen the law is basically a scheme of interpretation. One main challenge of a theory of law is, therefore, to explain what this scheme of interpretation consists in. The aim is to explain what makes us construe certain actions and events in the world as having legal meaning, and what this legal meaning consists in. The first question is the question about the conditions of legal validity, and the second is the question about the meaning of the normativity of law. Both, however, concern the sphere of meaning; a philosophical account of the nature of law is an account of the collective, public, and, to some extent objective, meaning of some social reality. In this respect, law is very much like a natural language, and we can say that philosophy of law is analogous to the philosophy of this language, as it were. Therefore, it makes no more sense to offer a reduction of philosophy of law to sociology as it would make sense to reduce philosophy of language to sociology. This, I believe, was one of Kelsen's most important arguments; so let me explain it in some detail.

---

[25] GT, 175. By the term "normative jurisprudence" Kelsen meant the philosophical account of legal norms—not normative in the sense of prescriptive.

The idea that philosophy of law can and should be replaced by some scientific-type theory has been simmering in jurisprudence, mostly American (and Scandinavian) jurisprudence, at least since the early 1900s. This trend of "naturalizing jurisprudence," as Brian Leiter calls it, can be understood in two different ways, however, and Kelsen's objections apply, as they should, only to one of them. Let us call them *reductive-displacement* and *agenda-displacement* theories. A reductive-displacement theory takes a certain realm or object of inquiry—call it *O*—as given, and that is currently explained by a certain type of theory—call it theory of type *A*—and purports to offer a reduction of the theory of *O* to a different type of theory—call it *B*. In other words, the reductive-displacement view purports to replace an *A*-type theory of *O* with a *B*-type theory of *O*. This is the kind of reductive displacement that Kelsen claims to be impossible with respect to jurisprudence. An agenda-displacement view, on the other hand, does not purport to offer a reduction of one type of theory to another, but primarily to shift the relevant research agenda. Such a view regards *the object of inquiry* in need of displacement and, only consequently, the kind of theory that is deemed appropriate.

I think that we can best explain the distinction and its significance by taking a closer look at the American legal realist school of thought that thrived during the first few decades of the twentieth century. Our interest, however, will be confined to American legal realism as a model of displacement theories; I will not attempt to provide a detailed historical survey of this school of thought or to scrutinize in detail any particular version of it (and there were many). It would be safe to say, however, that all the various versions of American legal realism shared a commitment to the following framework argument:[26]

(1) *Law is, ultimately, what the courts in fact do.*

(1a) Therefore, to know what the law is, one needs to be able to predict what the courts will in fact do.

(2) *Legal norms do not provide sufficiently determinate grounds for prediction of what the courts will in fact do.*

---

[26] The basic ideas of this framework were already present in Oliver Wendell Holmes Jr.'s famous lecture "The Path of the Law."

(3)   *Therefore, some other type of theory is needed that will enable more accurate predictions of judicial decisions.*

(3a) The kind of theory that is needed for such predictions can only be a scientific theory, empirical in nature, about the ways in which judges actually reach their decisions.

(4)   *Therefore, jurisprudence has to be replaced by empirical-scientific theory of some sort.*

Brian Leiter was quite right to argue that there are two ways to understand this methodological argument, mostly depending on how one understands the first premise.[27] If the first premise is understood as a conceptual, philosophical claim about the nature of law, it is obviously false, and then the whole argument is rendered incoherent. I also agree with Leiter that there is a much better way to understand the argument that easily avoids this incoherence. So let us see what is going on here. There is certainly some plausibility in the view that if one wants to know what *the law* on this or that issue really is (in a given jurisdiction), one would need to consult the content of judicial decisions. It is, indeed, a necessary feature of any legal order that some people must determine how the law applies to particular cases. And there is a sense in which this determination of what the law means in this or that particular case is the real, or true, content of the law. Thus the focus on actual judicial decisions is not, by itself, necessarily misguided. The question is: focus for what purposes? What exactly is the question we answer by saying that *the law is* what judges in fact say that it is?

Critics, such as H.L.A. Hart, were quick to point out that if we understand the first premise of the framework argument as an answer to the philosophical question about the nature of law, it makes no sense. Hart argued that it makes no sense to say that the law is, generally, what judges in fact decide, because people's institutional role qua judges is *constituted* by the law. We first need laws that establish judicial roles before people can make any

---

[27] In this section I rely mostly on Leiter's "Legal Realism"; Leiter has developed his views in greater detail in the essays collected in his *Naturalizing Jurisprudence*. Some of the essays in that volume seem to be much more sympathetic to the "naturalization" of jurisprudence than this older article would imply.

decisions in their official, judicial capacity. And there is a great deal of law that has to be in place, as it were, and generally understood as legal material, before we can come to grasp the decisions of judges as having the legal significance and the legal ramifications that they do.[28]

Now, you might think that the legal realists have just made a silly mistake. But in all likelihood, the mistake may lie elsewhere; it may be a mistake to attribute to the realists the kind of philosophical interest in the nature of law that gives rise to the incoherence of the framework argument. In other words, the first premise of the argument should not be taken to assert the rather absurd thesis that law, generally speaking, is what judges do in fact (as Hart seems to have assumed). Instead of seeing this point as an answer to the philosophical question of "what is law?" we may see it as an expression of a particular research interest—a suggested research agenda that focuses on prediction of judicial decisions. And if we construe the first premise of the framework argument in terms of a declaration of a research agenda, no incoherence would be involved. To put the matter simply, the realists were not interested in the philosophy of law. They just wanted to set a new research agenda, an agenda that focuses on the kinds of tools we need to be able to determine how judges reach their decisions, and what would enable us to predict the kinds of decisions they are likely to make in the future. Generally speaking, then, the kind of displacement theory that the realists were after is not the reductive kind, but the kind I've called agenda-displacement theory.

Clear evidence for this interpretation of the realists' project can be gained from realizing that the second premise of the methodological argument would make no sense without it. The second premise asserts that legal norms do not provide sufficiently determinate grounds for prediction of what the courts will in fact do. As the realists were at pains to show, judicial decisions are often reached on the basis of judges' instinctive reactions to the facts of the cases they face, using the legal material as a rationalization of their decisions rather than grounds of it. This thesis can

[28] See Hart, *The Concept of Law*, 133. (Unless otherwise indicated, all references are to the first edition.)

only make sense, however, if we already possess a certain conception of what legal norms are and how they differ from any other grounds on which judges can rely to reach their decisions.[29] To suggest, as the realists have tirelessly argued, that legal norms do not provide *sufficient* constraints on judicial decisions, entails a necessary, albeit implicit, recognition that some account of what legal norms are, and how they differ from other possible constraints on deliberation, must be available. In other words, the second premise entails that legal norms are distinguishable from other types of potential constraints on judicial decision-making. Leiter argued, quite plausibly I think, that by and large the legal realists were quite aware of this, and they simply assumed that something like traditional legal positivism provides an adequate answer to the question of what legal norms are and what makes them legal. They were not interested in providing a competing account to this conceptual thesis about the nature of law. Their interests simply lay elsewhere.

Now perhaps we can see how the point generalizes: The case of legal realism can explain Kelsen's dictum that "sociology can define the phenomenon of law, the positive law of a particular community, only by having recourse to the concept of law as defined by normative jurisprudence. Sociological jurisprudence presupposes this concept." In other words, Kelsen would have no objection to the kind of agenda-displacement theory that the American legal realists were after, as long as it is understood that such a theory does not purport to replace jurisprudence with sociology or any other "natural" science. Moreover, Kelsen would have agreed that such a methodological displacement theory actually presupposes that there is some philosophical account available to explain how legal sources differ from other types of constraints on decisions of judges and legal officials. Naturalizing jurisprudence, to use Leiter's expression, works fine as long as it is not really jurisprudence—understood as the philosophical question about the nature of law—that one attempts to reduce to a natural science. The philosophical question about the nature of

---

[29] Again, this is a point that had been observed by Hart, ibid.; and see Leiter, "Legal Realism."

law is one about a scheme of interpretation; it is a question about the collective meaning and self-understandings of a complex social reality. A scientific interest about ways in which judges reach their decisions, psychologically, sociologically, or otherwise, is a worthwhile project. But it is just not the kind of project that could possibly explain what constitutes a judicial role in the legal sense of it, or what constitutes a legal norm as opposed to other types of sources that may or may not affect judges' decisions.

SUGGESTED FURTHER READINGS

George, *Natural Law Theory*.
Hart, *Essays on Jurisprudence*, chap. 4.
Kelsen, *General Theory of Law and State*.
———, *Pure Theory of Law*.
Llewellyn, *Jurisprudence: Realism in Theory and Practice*.
Raz, *The Authority of Law*, chaps. 3–8, 16.
———, *The Concept of a Legal System*.

Social Rules at the Foundations of Law

KELSEN'S INFLUENCE on H.L.A. Hart's seminal work in legal philosophy, *The Concept of Law*, might not be readily apparent to a casual reader. A substantial part of the book is devoted to a detailed criticism of John Austin's command theory of law, while Kelsen's work is hardly mentioned. In this chapter I want to show that Hart's theory of law takes Kelsen's foundation to its reasonable conclusions, relying on some of Kelsen's best insights but amending them in some crucial aspects. In particular, Kelsen's failure to provide a nonreductive explanation of legal validity is a lesson that Hart carefully learned. His theory of law is reductive all the way through. The reductive explanation that Hart offered is not confined to the explication of legal validity; it extends to a quasi-sociological account of the normativity of law as well. Hart's extensive critical focus on Austin creates the impression that he found Austin's reductive definition of law profoundly inadequate. That is true, but Hart's main argument with Austin is not about reductionism per se; it aims to show that the particular reduction that Austin offered uses the wrong building blocks. Instead of trying to reduce law to a sociological conception of sovereignty, as Austin suggested, Hart offers a more nuanced and complex picture that puts the idea of social rules at the foundations of law.

The chapter proceeds as follows: In the first part I will briefly present Hart's critique of Austin's theory of law, focusing on two main themes—that law is not comprised of commands, and that law does not necessarily emanate from the political sovereign. In the second part I will show that Hart's alternative to Austin is a reductive version of Kelsen's theory of the basic norm. Finally, I will point out some of the difficulties in Hart's account of the normativity of law, suggesting some avenues that will be pursued in subsequent chapters.

Why Law Is Not the Command of the Sovereign

Commands

A long tradition in jurisprudence, dating back to the political philosophy of Thomas Hobbes, sees the law as the tool of political sovereignty. Law is the means by which the political sovereign rules and directs the conduct of its subjects. It is all too easy to dismiss this conception as anachronistic. Does it not assume that the political sovereign is like an absolute monarch, sitting on his throne issuing commands to his subjects to do this or refrain from doing that? Surely a modern legal system is more complex than that, and it is doubtful that law has ever been quite so simple. Let us not be so dismissive. The command theory of law is based on two powerful insights. First, it assumes, quite plausibly, that laws consist of instructions or directives issued by some people in order to direct the conduct of others. Now, of course, there are many contexts in which some people tell other people what to do or how to behave. What makes action-guiding instructions legal has to do with the origins and the function of the guidance: If the guidance emanates from the political sovereign and purports to function as an exercise of sovereignty, then it is law. Recall our first example about the use of mobile phones while driving: What makes it the law in California these days that one has to use a hands-free device? Surely, as we have seen, it is not the content of the directive. What makes it a legal norm is the fact that the requirement has been issued, in the appropriate way, by the California legislature in its legislative capacity. So perhaps this is all there is to it: Instructions or commands of the political sovereign are what we call law.

This is the basic insight that Austin tried to work out.[1] The insight has two main components: that law always has the form of a command, and that it necessarily originates from the political

[1] Austin, *The Province of Jurisprudence Determined*.

sovereign. Hart found both of these components fraught with difficulties. Only a small fraction of the law may be said to consist of commands; and, more importantly, we cannot explicate the sources of law in terms of political sovereignty because the very idea or concept of sovereignty is a juridical one. Law partly constitutes our conceptions of sovereignty; it cannot be reduced to it. I will take up these two points in turn.

According to Austin, each and every legal norm is a *command*, namely, the expression of a wish by a person (or persons), that some others behave in a certain way, backed by a threat of sanction: "Do this or else. . . ." In chapter 3 of *The Concept of Law*, Hart explains in great detail that most laws are not of the kind that can be reduced to the form of "Do this or else. . . ." The two main and closely related problems with the "Do this or else . . ." model of laws are, first, that the model assumes that laws are there to impose obligations ("do/don't do . . ."); and second, it assumes that every legal norm is backed by a threat of sanction ("or else . . ."). And of course, these two aspects are very closely related; together they form the idea of a command.

Hart acknowledges that some laws have this kind of structure. Clear examples are the main provisions of a criminal code, imposing obligations to refrain from certain modes of conduct, backed by the threat of punishment if one does not comply. But, as Hart rightly pointed out, most of the law is not really like that. A great many laws are not there to impose an obligation.[2] For example, laws often confer a *legal power*. They prescribe manners in which an agent may introduce a change in the preexisting normative relations that obtain.[3] Consider the formation of a contract, for example. A contract is formed by an offer and the acceptance of the offer. Laws determine what constitutes an offer, an acceptance of it, and the legal ramifications that follow from

---

[2] To be a bit more accurate, we should acknowledge that in contemporary legal systems, a huge amount of administrative legal regulation takes the form of "do this or else." Many of these regulatory legal norms are enacted by administrative agencies.

[3] Hart, *The Concept of Law*, 27–35. The definition of "legal power" that Hart adopted comes from W. N. Hohfeld's influential analysis of legal rights; see his *Fundamental Legal Conceptions*.

the formation of contractual relations of various kinds. The laws that determine how a legally binding contract is formed do not have the structure of "do this or else"; the law is not in the business of obligating anyone to form a contract—neither to make an offer nor to accept one. The structure of such norms is entirely conditional: *If* you want to form a legally binding contract, this is *how* it is done. But again, you do not have to make a legal offer or to accept one. In other words, the law here does not impose any obligation; it confers a power—the power to create a new set of rights and duties that would be legally recognized.

As Hart admits, however, Austin was not unaware of this problem. Nevertheless, he maintained that the "do this or else . . ." model applies to all laws, albeit often indirectly. The laws that prescribe modes of forming a contract, for example, in effect tell the subjects: Do this . . . or else your attempt to form a legally binding contract would fail. True, there is no straightforward sanction for noncompliance that looms here. But there is this "or else": You fail to accomplish the legal consequences you may have wanted to achieve. The sanction, so to speak, consists in the *legal nullity* of your action. Hart found this solution very inadequate, and for two main reasons.

First, Hart observed that there is a conceptual distinction between norms that tell you "do this . . . or else," and norms that constitute or determine ways of creating new normative relations such as a rule that confers a power to make a contract. In the former case, there is a clear distinction between the action requirement and the sanction element that would be applied in case one fails to perform. We can fully understand the action requirement without the sanction element. In the latter case, however, no such distinction is possible. A rule that determines what counts as a valid contract only makes sense on the basis of the assumption that, without complying with the rule, you have not formed a valid contract. We just cannot separate the action requirement from the legal nullity as a consequence of noncompliance.[4]

Second, Austin's rejoinder fails to notice that there is a very important difference between the function of a law that purports

[4] Hart, *The Concept of Law*, 34–35.

to impose an obligation, such as the obligation not to murder or to steal, and the function of a power-conferring law. The main function of the latter is not to impose any obligations, not even obliquely or indirectly. The law is simply not in the business of telling people how to behave; it is in the business of providing a service.[5] But then the question is: What kind of service? Is it not the service of having one's rights secured by the coercive powers of the law?

Think about it this way: Why would parties to a transaction care whether their exchange of promises is legally recognized as a contract? A very plausible answer is that they care about it because they would want to have the enforcement services of the law at their disposal in case something goes wrong. And this is precisely how Kelsen saw it. He shared Hart's view that Austin's command model is too simplistic, failing to see the major role that power-conferring norms serve in the law. However, Kelsen shared Austin's view that law's enforcing mechanisms, its ability to compel behavior by the use of force, is what makes the law a unique instrument of social control. Consequently, Kelsen came up with a rather counterintuitive analysis of legal norms, whereby all legal norms are ultimately addressed to officials, instructing them to use force if certain conditions obtain. Under this conception, the kinds of norms we would normally regard as individual legal norms (such as a norm that determines what counts as a contract, or a norm prohibiting murder, and so forth) are actually just fragments of laws, part of a list of conditions addressed to officials determining when the use of force will be mandated. All laws are instructions to officials of the form: "If conditions $C_{1 \ldots n}$ obtain, use force against Y to compel result X." Thus, Kelsen seems to have shared Austin's view that laws are basically commands or instructions, but the commands are ultimately addressed to those who may use force to compel behavior.[6]

---

[5] Ibid., 33–35.

[6] Kelsen, GT, 63. Kelsen did not actually invent this idea of laws as fragments of instructions to officials; the idea originates with Bentham, *An Introduction to the Principles of Morals and Legislation*, 330ff.

Understandably, Hart did not find it difficult to ridicule Kelsen's analysis of legal norms. Kelsen's analysis misses the crucial point that the main function of most legal norms is to actually *guide* the conduct of the law's subjects. The law is there to provide reasons for its subjects to behave in certain ways, not to tell officials when to use force to compel behavior. Hart demonstrated this point by the distinction between a tax and a fine. In both cases, the instruction to the relevant officials is the same: If conditions $C_{1 \ldots n}$ obtain, extract $\$X$ from Y. But there is this crucial difference: When the law imposes the penalty of a fine, its main aim is to discourage the type of conduct in question, and the fine would be extracted only if the law failed in its main objective—to prevent people from doing whatever it is for which they may be fined. Contrary to this, taxes are typically not meant to discourage the type of conduct for which one is taxed. Income tax is not meant to instruct people to refrain from gaining income—quite the opposite. Thus Hart concludes that Kelsen's analysis of legal norms in terms of instructions addressed to officials is obviously flawed since it misses entirely the main action-guiding function that most laws have.[7]

It may be worth pausing here for a while to see what exactly this debate about the nature of legal norms is about. And it is not about one thing; there are at least three different questions that are entangled in this debate among Austin, Kelsen, and Hart. Partly, this is a debate about the main functions of law in society and how closely those functions are tied to the use of force, and law's ability to impose sanctions; partly, it is a debate about the question of whether laws are essentially instructions addressed by some people to others; and partly, though least importantly, the debate is about the question of whether all legal norms can be reduced to one general form.

Undoubtedly, Hart was right about the third point. Both Austin's assumption that laws are basically commands of the form "do this . . . or else," and Kelsen's suggestion to see all laws as a list of instructions to officials when and how to use force, suffer from

---

[7] Hart, *The Concept of Law*, 35–41. (This is one of the only places in *The Concept of Law* where Hart explicitly refers to Kelsen.)

the same flaw of oversimplification (or "distortion as the price of uniformity," as Hart called it[8]). In every developed legal system, there are many different types of norms, and there is no reason to assume that all those types can be reduced to one basic model. But the other two questions are much more complicated. Consider, first, the idea of sanctions: Austin and Kelsen share the view that there is a very intimate connection between law's ability to impose sanctions for noncompliance and the main functions of law in society. They share the view that it is this element of using force to compel compliance that makes the law a unique normative system. As Kelsen explicitly stated, the main function of law in our societies is to monopolize the use of force.[9] And although Kelsen does not quite say it, I think that he shared Austin's view that law is essentially an instrument of political sovereignty. Undoubtedly, this view belongs to a long tradition in political thought emanating from Hobbes, which regards the main rationale of political sovereignty in terms of monopolizing the use of force in order to pacify society and ensure peaceful coexistence of individuals. To a considerable extent, Hart's arguments in *The Concept of Law* are meant to challenge this Hobbesian tradition in jurisprudence. The challenge is twofold. One concerns the variety of legal norms and their different social functions. The second line of criticism, as we shall see shortly, concerns the tight connection that the Hobbesian tradition in jurisprudence forged between law and political sovereignty. I will argue that both of these challenges are very important, but neither of them is entirely successful. Let me first consider the role of sanctions in understanding the functions of law in society. Later we will discuss Hart's challenge to the idea that law is an instrument of political sovereignty.

The role of sanctions in the law and the use of force, Hart maintained, was greatly exaggerated by Austin and Kelsen. A closer attention to the various functions of different types of legal norms and institutions would show that the law does not always need an element of sanction in order to fulfill its functions. Let us be careful not to misunderstand the debate here. Hart's main

[8] Ibid., 33.
[9] Kelsen, GT, 18–19.

point is not about human nature; it is not about the question of whether most people are essentially law abiding and would normally follow the law without being threatened by sanctions. Although Hart also thought that, indeed, most people in a civilized legal system would normally want to know what the law requires in order to do the right thing, and the threat of sanction is less important than traditional Hobbesians might think, this is not the main issue. The main question is about something that is more central to philosophy of law: What are the kinds of problems and needs that law is there to solve or respond to, and are they tied so closely to law's coercive aspect as the Hobbesian tradition would have it? In other words, the question is how central the element of force is to the functions law serves in our social lives. Perhaps we would be better served here by an argument Joseph Raz suggested in support of Hart's position about this issue.[10]

Raz asks us to entertain the following thought experiment: Let us imagine a world in which no element of sanction would be required. Let us assume that there is a world of angels, as it were, which is identical to our world, with only this difference: Whatever it is in our world that requires the law to threaten with sanctions for noncompliance does not prevail with respect to the angels. Now the relevant question is this: Would this world of angels need various institutions that would resemble the kinds of institutions we call *law* in our society? If the answer is affirmative, we should conclude that the functions of law are not so closely tied to law's sanction element as the Hobbesian tradition maintains. And Raz's answer is that, indeed, we should be able to see that there are a great many institutions that even angels would need that look very much like the kinds of institutions we call law around here. For example, the angels would need normative solutions to large-scale coordination problems; they would need mechanisms for determining what needs to be done in circumstances where reasonable angels may disagree, but some kind of a collective decision is required; they would need mechanisms for resolving conflicting views between individuals about such matters; and they would need institutions entrusted with

[10] See Raz's *Practical Reason and Norms*, 158–60.

determining the relevant facts in conflictual circumstances, and the like.[11] Thus, Raz concludes, with Hart, that the law's coercive element—its ability to use force to compel compliance—is much less important than people tend to think. Even without the need to use force, there are many needs and functions that legal institutions and various legal norms serve for us.

I am not entirely convinced by this thought experiment. Although I find its conclusion generally correct, the argument underestimates the importance of the coercive element of law. Recent advances in game theory in economics and cognitive psychology have shown that there are countless situations in which rational people have a very strong incentive to act against their own self-interest as well as against the common good. One of the main functions of law, manifest in a great variety of legal arrangements, is to solve these kinds of problems by compelling individuals to overcome their initial incentive to defect from cooperative behavior or to act against their own long-term self-interest.[12] By threatening with sanctions for noncompliance, the law is able to provide a service for the parties concerned: It enables them to behave cooperatively, generally in the agents' best interest, in spite of their rational incentive to do the contrary. As an example, consider the case of taxes. It is in our own interest, as well as the common good, to have people pay taxes that enable the production of goods and services that are important and otherwise could not be produced. However, each potential taxpayer has a very strong rational incentive to defect; from the perspective of each individual, the best outcome is achieved if most others pay the taxes while they do not. And since every individual knows this about themselves and the others, everybody's incentive to pay is hugely diminished by the fear that others have a strong incentive to defect

---

[11] Notice that the need for these institutions suggests the need for both legislative and adjudicative institutions, very similar to what we regard as legislation and adjudication in our world.

[12] It is not my intention to imply that game theory models provide the best framework for analyzing such cases. These models tend to be framed in terms of an individual's subjective preferences, and they take preferences as given, without any concern for reasons for action and responsiveness to reasons.

as well. By compelling everybody to pay taxes with the threat of sanction, the law ensures that our rational self-interest is attained.

The problem with Raz's thought experiment is that it is crucially ambiguous about this issue, because the outcome depends on how we define the rationality of the angels. If we define their rationality in ways that would make them susceptible to the relevant kind of rationality failures that we have, the conclusion would be that "law" in a world of angels would also need to incorporate some sanction elements. Yet if we define the rationality of the angels to exclude such failures, then it becomes very unclear how much we can learn from this thought experiment. A world of such perfectly rational angels might be just too remote from ours to warrant any significant conclusions about the functions of law in our society. The conclusion I am heading toward is that the truth about the importance of the sanction element of law is somewhere in between the Austin and Kelsen view and that of Hart and Raz. No doubt the latter are right that it is a mistake to forge too tight a connection between law's ability to use force to compel compliance with the main functions of law in society. But we should be careful not to overstate this mistake; even if not all, a great many functions of law in solving the kinds of problems it is there to solve are made possible by its ability to change people's incentives and compel behavior by the threat of sanctions.

The Sovereign

According to Austin, what makes normative instructions distinctively legal consists, first and foremost, in the origins of the instruction. If, and only if, the command or instruction emanates from the political sovereign, then it is legal. Since Austin's theory of law is categorically reductive, he had to offer a definition of sovereignty that is given in nonjuridical terms. After all, the whole point of Austin's theory is to give an explanation of law in terms of something else, more basic and factual in nature. And it is precisely this attempt to reduce law to facts of a non-normative kind that renders Austin's theory a paradigmatic example of legal positivism. Thus, Austin defined political sovereignty in sociological terms, consisting in social facts about habits of obedience: A person, or group of persons, who is *habitually obeyed* by a certain population and not in the habit of obeying anyone else, is the political sovereign.[13]

An objection immediately comes to mind: Isn't the very idea of obedience a normative one? To say that one person *obeys* another typically implies that the person being obeyed is in a normative position or has the authority to instruct the other under the circumstances. But this is not a serious worry. There is nothing wrong with the use of "obedience" to describe a situation where one person does what the other tells her to do, without any hierarchical or authoritative relations between them. The word "obey" can be used in purely factual (that is, non-normative) terms, and this is how Austin must have intended it.[14]

Hart's main difficulty with the characterization of sovereignty in terms of habits of obedience is different: Hart's argument aims to show that the idea of sovereignty is, essentially, a juridical one.[15] Sovereignty cannot be at the foundations of law because it is partly the law that constitutes what sovereignty is and who counts as the particular sovereign in any given population. I will not describe in detail Hart's argument. The basic intuition that lies behind it, however, is not difficult to explain. Think about the law as a kind of a game in which there is only one basic rule: We do whatever The Leader tells us to do. Would it make sense to say that the game *consists in* what the particular person, say *X*, who happens to be The Leader, commands? Surely the appropriate description is that the game consists in what *X as* The Leader tells us to do. Which means that first we need some rules that constitute the role of The Leader, and rules that determine how *X* becomes one, before we can ascribe to the commands of *X* the

---

[13] Austin, *The Province of Jurisprudence Determined.*

[14] It is perfectly OK, for example, to say that *X* habitually obeys the neighborhood bully, without implying that the bully is somehow authorized to terrorize *X*. And even when we say, for example, that an object that falls from my desk to the floor "obeys the laws of gravitation," perhaps we use the word "obey" somewhat figuratively, but it is not a terrible stretch.

[15] Hart, *The Concept of Law,* chap. 4.

significance that they have in this game. This, I think, is the basic argument that lies behind Hart's objection to Austin's theory of law.

The game analogy is not a coincidence. It is one that Hart himself often used, and for good reason: It is evident in our practices of playing games that rules have a foundational, that is, constitutive, status. Games typically have rules about what a player is required to do, or may or may not do; but this is only part of the story. In addition to this regulative function of rules, the rules of the game *constitute* what the game is, and the various roles that participants in the game have. And, at least in this respect, law is very much like a game. Before anyone can be said to have issued a legal instruction or a command, there must first be some rules that constitute the role of that person to make the kind of move that would have the legal significance that it does.

One may wonder, however, whether Austin would disagree. After all, he did suggest that sovereignty is constituted by the habits of obedience that prevail in a given population. If there is a certain population that is in a habit of obeying X, and X himself is not in the habit of obeying anyone else, then, and only then, X is the sovereign. So perhaps a plausible interpretation of Austin would be that general habits of obedience constitute what sovereignty is. How is it different from Hart's insistence that sovereignty, just like the role of the umpire in a game, is a role that is constituted by rules? Hart has two related answers. First, he claims that the tools Austin provides would not be sufficient to explain even the simplest form of a legal transition from one person qua sovereign to another. Suppose X is a sovereign in society S, by meeting Austin's definition; but then X passes away and Y takes over as the legal successor to X, and is now the lawful sovereign in S. Surely, at the first stages of Y's rule, it cannot be said that Y enjoys a *habit of obedience* by members of S. Habits take time to evolve. Now, of course we all understand what would make Y the legal successor to X: Legal systems tend to have rules of transition and continuity that determine such matters—such as who gets to replace X in his legal-political role when X can no longer function as the sovereign. But there seems to be nothing in Austin's account of sovereignty to explain how such rules of transition are possible. Surely they cannot be constituted by habits of obedience, as there are none, at least not for a while.[16]

Second, and this may lie at the heart of the previous problem as well, Austin missed the crucial distinction between a mere *regularity of behavior* and an instance of *following a rule*. A habit of obedience is a regularity of behavior. Many things we do regularly, however, are not necessarily instances of following a rule. We regularly eat lunch, or frequently go to a movie, and so forth, but there is no rule that requires such conduct. In eating lunch, one does not follow a rule. Reasons for action may occur in some regular fashion, and when we comply with such reasons, we exhibit a regular pattern of behavior. When we follow a rule, however, we regard the rule itself as a reason for doing what it requires. Rules have a normative significance; the existence of the rule is something that figures in our practical reasoning, it is something that counts in favor of doing what the rule requires.

Thus Hart's critique of Austin is twofold. First, Austin failed to recognize that sovereignty is an institution, and institutions are constituted by rules. Second, he failed to recognize that rules are not merely regularities of behavior. These two points, taken together, are aimed to show that it is not possible to offer a reductive explanation of legal validity in terms of a sociological conception of sovereignty. Let me be clear about Hart's argument: Hart does not need to deny that it is possible to come up with a definition of political sovereignty that is purely sociological, as it were. The point is that no such characterization of sovereignty would capture the kind of sovereignty that we are after, namely, the kind that explains the role of the sovereign as a source of law, as the kind of entity whose directives constitute legal norms. In order to get the relevant kind of sovereignty—that is, to identify the agents whose actions or decisions create the law—one would first need to know the rules that constitute sovereignty as a legally significant entity, the kind of entity or institution generally recognized to be the source of legal norms. In other words, what we need is

---

[16] See Hart, *The Concept of Law*, chap. 4.

an institutional account of sovereignty, and such an account must be based on rules that constitute the institution. Second, as noted, rules are not merely regularities of behavior. The fact, if it is one, that there is a habit—a regularity of behavior—in accordance with X's instructions would not be sufficient to explain what makes X the political sovereign in the relevant sense. What we need, Hart concludes, is "the idea of a rule, without which we cannot hope to elucidate even the most elementary forms of law."[17]

Notice that there is one crucial respect in which Hart and Kelsen agree here. They both share the view that we need some normative framework already in place before we can come to interpret certain actions or events to have the legal significance that they do. For Kelsen, this normative framework is provided by the presupposition of the basic norm. Hart, as we shall see in a moment, retains Austin's reductive methodology and seeks to provide the requisite normative framework in terms of the idea of social rules. In other words, Hart employs the idea of social rules to serve the same theoretical functions that Kelsen ascribed to the basic norm. But his account of social rules remains, quite self-consciously, a reductive one. It is not Austin's methodology that Hart rejects—only the building blocks that form the foundations of law. The following section takes up the details of this account.

How Is Law Constituted by Social Rules?

Hart begins his account of the nature of law by introducing a distinction between *primary* and *secondary* rules.[18] Primary rules prescribe certain modes of conduct, such as "Do this . . ." or "Don't do that. . . ." Their object is the guidance of behavior. Secondary rules are rules about rules: They take other rules as their object and guide ways in which rules can be created, modified, or abolished, or ways in which interpretation of rules is to

---

[17] Hart, *The Concept of Law*, 78.
[18] Ibid., 78–79.

be adjudicated, and such. Hart employs this distinction for two purposes. His first purpose is to show that in every developed legal system there are rules of both kinds. Every legal system would have, in addition to its primary rules of conduct, a whole range of secondary rules prescribing ways in which other rules may be created, modified, or interpreted. (In fact, power-conferring rules, like those discussed in the previous section, are of such secondary nature.) So this is another nail in the coffin of Austin's command model of law; commands are primary rules of conduct. But the law must contain, in addition to such primary rules, many kinds of secondary rules that are not directed to guide conduct but to enable various agents to create new norms or modify existing ones.

The second purpose of the introduction of secondary rules is to show how rules can constitute legal institutions. There is, Hart famously claimed, in every community that has a legal system, a special kind of secondary rules, which he calls *rules of recognition*—rules that identify certain types of actions or events as the kinds of actions or events that create law in that community. In the existence of such rules of recognition, Hart says, we find "the germ of the idea of legal validity."[19] The rules of recognition are social rules that a community follows in identifying ways in which law is created, modified, or abolished, that is, these are the rules that constitute what counts as sources of legally valid norms in a given community.[20] As we have already seen in the previous chapter, a legal chain of validity always comes to an end. In every legal system we reach a point where some account must be given, in nonlegal terms, to explain what grants certain actions and events the legal significance that they have. There must be something more basic or foundational that grounds the very idea of legality. If, as Hart suggests, rules ground the idea

---

[19] Ibid., 93.

[20] My formulation in the text is not entirely accurate: Hart identified three main types of secondary rules that legal systems would have: rules of recognition, rules of change, and rules of adjudication. Perhaps I am including in the rules of recognition elements Hart classified under the rules of change. Nothing in my subsequent argument depends on this question of classification, however.

of legality, then those rules must be more foundational than the legal institutions that are constituted by them—hence the idea of social rules.

Hart also maintained that because various rules of recognition might come into conflict, legal systems would typically have provisions for some order of superiority, whereby some sources of law are subordinate to others (for example, state law is subordinate to federal law; judicial decisions might be subordinate to legislation, and the like). In other words, rules of recognition would typically manifest a hierarchical structure subsumed under one main or *master* rule of recognition. The idea that legal systems are hierarchically structured is familiar from Kelsen's theory of legal systems and his postulates about the basic norm. We discussed this in chapter 1, and the same doubts we had about the idea that in every legal system there is one basic norm should apply to Hart's rule of recognition as well. It is probably an oversimplification to assume that in every legal system there is one master rule of recognition. More plausibly, there are several rules of recognition, and the potential conflicts between them are not necessarily resolved.

No other idea is more closely associated with Hart's theory of law than the idea that legality is constituted by social rules of recognition. The novelty in Hart's account, however, consists in the idea that these are *social* rules. The theoretical function of the rules of recognition is basically the same as the function ascribed by Kelsen to the basic norm. The difference between Hart's rule of recognition and Kelsen's basic norm is only a difference in the nature of these norms. For Kelsen, as we have seen, it is a presupposition; for Hart, it is an actual social norm followed by a given community. There is one point where Hart explicitly draws this contrast between the rules of recognition and the basic norm, and it is worth quoting in full:

> Some writers, who have emphasized the legal ultimacy of the rule of recognition, have expressed this by saying that, whereas the legal validity of other rules of the system can be demonstrated by reference to it, its own validity cannot

be demonstrated but is "assumed" or "postulated" or is a "hypothesis." This may, however, be seriously misleading.

And then Hart explains what is misleading about the idea that the rule of recognition/basic norm is "postulated" or presupposed:

> First, a person who seriously asserts the validity of some given rule of law . . . himself makes use of a rule of recognition which *he accepts* as appropriate for identifying the law. Secondly, it is the case that this rule of recognition . . . is not only accepted by him but is *the rule of recognition actually accepted and employed* in the general operation of the system. If the truth of this presupposition were doubted, it could be *established by reference to actual practice: to the way in which courts identify what is to count as law, and to the general acceptance of or acquiescence in these identifications.*[21] (Emphasis mine)

I hope that we can now see very clearly that Hart generally accepts Kelsen's theory of the basic norm, while explicitly rejecting its antireductionist underpinning. As we have seen in the previous chapter, Kelsen was under pressure to concede that the content of the basic norm is determined by social practice. Hart draws the same conclusion, which for him simply means that the whole idea of presupposing the basic norm is redundant. Once we recognize, as we should, that in identifying the sources of law, judges and other officials follow certain rules, those rules need not be presupposed. They are actual social rules followed and thus "accepted" by the relevant community. In other words, Hart's idea of the rule of recognition is essentially the idea of Kelsen's basic norm characterized reductively in terms of social facts that prevail in a given community. The relevant social facts, as we shall see in a moment, are facts about people's conduct, beliefs, and attitudes.

What Hart needs, therefore, is a detailed account of what social rules are, and how social rules can ground both the ideas of legal validity and the normativity we ascribe to law. Hart's answer

---

[21] Hart, *The Concept of Law*, 105.

to these questions, given by what has come to be called the *practice theory of rules*, remains reductive all the way through:

A social rule, say R, exists in a population S, Hart maintained, if and only if the following conditions obtain:

(1) Most members of S *regularly conform* in their behavior to the content of R, and

(2) most members of S *accept R* as a rule, which means that

(a) for most members of S, the existence of R constitutes a reason for action in accordance to R,

(b) and members of S tend to employ R and refer to it as grounds for exerting pressure on other members to conform to R and as grounds for criticizing deviations from conformity to R.[22]

As we can see, according to Hart, the existence of a social rule consists of actual patterns of *conduct, beliefs,* and *attitudes*: We have a social rule when there is a component of conduct or behavior—that is, the regular conformity with the rule or the regularity of conduct in accordance with it; and a complex component of "acceptance" of the rule, which consists of (1) a belief shared by the population that the existence of the rule provides them with a reason for action and (2) a shared attitude of a positive endorsement of the rule that is manifest in its use as grounds of exerting pressure on others to comply as well, or criticizing them when they do not. Clearly, this is a reductive account of social rules. It purports to explain what social rules are in terms of overt behavior in a given social group, accompanied by certain beliefs and attitudes actually entertained by (most) members of that group. Notice that this is also an aggregative account because it purports to explain a social phenomenon in terms of the conduct, beliefs, and attitudes of individual members of the relevant population. If most members of a given population behave in a certain way, and share some beliefs and attitudes with respect to that behavior, then we have "the idea of a rule," which is, according to Hart, the foundation of a legal system.

---

[22] Hart's explanation of the nature of social rules is scattered around several places in *The Concept of Law*. Most of the essential points are at 82–86.

This strong reductionism in Hart's account of social rules has been missed by many commentators, and partly due to a rather cryptic account Hart himself provided of various ways in which social rules can be observed and accounted for. Few pages in *The Concept of Law* generated more confusion than Hart's distinction between the *internal* and *external* aspects of rules.

"When a social group has certain rules of conduct," Hart says, it is possible to make different kinds of observations about the rules:

> It is possible to be concerned with the rules, either merely as an observer who does not himself accept them, or as a member of the group which accepts and uses them as guides to conduct.

The former is the external point of view and the latter the internal one. And then Hart immediately clarifies that the external point of view can be varied:

> For the observer may, without accepting the rules himself, assert that the group accepts the rules, and thus may from the outside refer to the way in which they are concerned with them from the internal point of view. [Or,] . . . we can if we choose to occupy the position of an observer who does not even refer in this way to the internal point of view of the group. Such an observer is content merely to record the regularities of observable behavior.[23]

Hart identifies three possible ways in which one can account for social rules: the internal point of view, which is the vantage point of members of the group who "accept" the rule—that is, regard the rule as reason for their action; an external point of view, which reports on the internal point of view without sharing the same beliefs and attitudes that members of the group do; and, what we can call an extreme external point of view, which only reports on the rules in terms of observable regularities of behavior. One can surmise that Hart's reason to mention the extreme version of the external point of view was, yet again, to show the flaws

[23] Hart, *The Concept of Law*, 87.

in Austin's simplistic reductionism. As mentioned earlier, Hart thought that Austin's definition of sovereignty in terms of habits of obedience is seriously flawed, partly because it does not recognize the crucial distinction between conformity to a regularity of behavior and instances of following a rule. It is as if Austin's characterization of sovereignty confines itself to an extreme external point of view, and thus is grossly inadequate for that reason alone. Any plausible account of social rules, Hart claims, must take into account the fact that people share the internal point of view. This is the point of view of the members of the group who regard the rules as binding—that is, for whom the rules provide reasons for action and reasons for exerting pressure on other members to comply as well.

If you recall Kelsen's discussion of the normativity of law, you might find it rather curious that Hart's distinctions seem less nuanced than Kelsen's. According to Hart, one can either describe social rules from the vantage point of a committed member, that is, from the vantage point of a person who regards the relevant rules as *binding* (reason-giving), or else one can report on such a point of view in the form of a report on others' conduct, beliefs, and attitudes. However, in addition to the internal point of view, which Kelsen clearly recognized as crucial to any account of a normative system, he had also recognized the possibility that one might deploy arguments about a normative system *as if* one accepts the internal point of view. Has Hart just failed to notice that there is this third possibility, the possibility of a *presumed* internal point of view or, as Raz has called it, detached normative statements?

It is possible that Hart just failed to notice that the distinctions he offered can be more fine-grained and that there is this possibility of making detached normative statements. But we should not lose sight of Hart's project and his aim in drawing these basic distinctions. And the main objective here is not, I think, a critique of Austin, but it is actually a critique of Kelsen. What Hart wants to show by these distinctions is not simply the importance of the internal point of view. His aim, I believe, was to show how the internal point of view can be accounted for in terms of people's beliefs and attitudes. In other words, the upshot of the distinction is about the *external* point of view, not the internal one. The contrast that Hart draws is between Austin's account, which he sees as an account that is confined to the extreme-external point of view, and his own, which is the account of an observer who "may, without accepting the rules himself, assert that the group accepts the rules, and thus may from the outside refer to the way in which *they* are concerned with them from the internal point of view."[24] Hart's aim is to lay the ground for a reductive account of social rules, one that explains the internal point of view in terms of people's behavior, beliefs, and attitudes. The fact that there is also the possibility of talking about social rules as if one regards them as binding is beside the point for these purposes. The point is to show that there is nothing amiss about explaining the normativity of a system of rules from the outside, as it were. We do not need to *presuppose* anything when we explain law's underlying normative framework. What we need is a kind of sociological account that explains the fact, the complex social fact, that people follow certain rules. And this account can be given, Hart claims, in terms of observing people's actual modes of conduct, the beliefs they have about their conduct, and their accompanying attitudes.

Let me try to sum this up. Hart clearly shares Kelsen's insight that the only way in which we can explain the idea of legality is by pointing to norms that grant certain types of actions and events the legal significance that we ascribe to them. There must be some norms that identify the ways in which law is created and modified in the relevant community. These are the *rules of recognition*. However, Hart does not share Kelsen's view that these norms have to be presupposed. The *rules of recognition* are social rules, actually followed (mostly) by judges and other legal officials, and, as such, can be observed and accounted for in terms of observing people's conduct, beliefs, and attitudes.

Some commentators have pointed out that there is an inherent difficulty in Hart's position: If the rules of recognition are, as Hart claims, the rules followed by judges and other officials, and that

---

[24] Ibid.

is how we would be able to identify them, how can those same rules constitute the role of such people *as* judges and officials? After all, it was Hart himself who repeatedly emphasized that we can only identify certain individuals qua judges or other legal officials on the basis of rules that confer the relevant legal powers on them and thus constitute their institutional roles. So it seems that we need some legal rules to explain who counts as "an official," but then we say that what counts as law is determined by the rules that those officials follow. Is there a chicken and egg problem here?[25] I do not think so. It is true that when Hart answers the question, whose rules the rules of recognition are? he points out that, mostly, they are the rules followed by judges and other legal officials. It is also true that Hart claims, and rightly so, that the role of such officials, qua officials, is itself constituted by rules. But there is no vicious circularity here. Consider, for example, the game of chess. As an activity of a particular kind—as a practice, if you will—chess is clearly constituted by its rules. Suppose you ask: *Whose* rules are they? The answer is, naturally, that these are rules followed by those who play the game—by chess players. And who is a chess player? Surely, the role of a chess player is also constituted by the rules of the game. You are a chess player if you play the game, that is, engage in the activity by following the rules of chess. Perhaps there is an air of paradox here, but there is no real paradox involved. When we have a set of rules that constitute a certain type of activity—such as playing chess or performing a theater play—the rules can constitute both the type of activity in question and the particular roles that people occupy within the activity. And, of course, the rules are those that are actually followed by the people who engage in the activity in question. In other words, the rules followed by those who play a particular institutional role can be the same rules that constitute the institutional role that forms part of an activity generally constituted by rules.[26]

---

[25] See Shapiro, "On Hart's Way Out."

[26] Perhaps part of the confusion stems from the fact that Hart seems to have assumed that constitutive rules are secondary rules—that is, rules about rules; and he clearly assumes that the rules of recognition are secondary rules. The chess example shows that, as a generalization, Hart erred here. The rules of chess are

None of this means that Hart's theory is unproblematic. Over the years, Hart's practice theory of social rules came under considerable pressure. There was a sense that Hart had not provided an explanation for the main element that would render the idea of rule-following rational or intelligible, namely, the reasons for following a rule. Hart's practice theory of rules seemed to provide only an account of what one would observe when a population follows a rule, namely, that people exhibit a regularity of behavior accompanied by some beliefs and attitudes they share about that regularity. But this account tells us nothing about the reasons people might have for following rules; Hart's account seems to be silent on the question of what makes it rational or intelligible for people to regard the relevant social norms as binding or obligatory. Strangely enough, it was Hart himself who gave us a very good reason to be concerned with this question (even though he must have thought that he provided us with reasons not to be concerned with this issue).

Consider a situation in which a gunman orders you to hand over your money or else he will shoot you. Clearly, this is not a legal order. But as Hart rightly pointed out, according to Austin's command theory of law, the only difference between the gunman's order and the orders of law consists in the fact that, as it happens, the gunman is not the political sovereign. Yet there is a clear sense, Hart claimed, that Austin's view misses something of crucial importance: It would be true to say that when faced with the gunman's order, the victim is "obliged" to hand over his money, but it would be wrong to suggest that the victim has "an obligation" or a "duty" to do so. However, unlike the gunman, the law often purports to create obligations; if a legal norm requires a certain type of conduct, the requirement purports to impose an *obligation* to comply.[27] And this is precisely the question about the normativity of law that we have sought all along: the question of how to explain this obligatory or binding element of legal norms.

---

not secondary rules; they are rules of conduct, specifying permissible and impermissible moves and their significance within the game. Nevertheless, the rules of chess are constitutive—they constitute what the game is.

[27] Hart, *The Concept of Law*, 80.

Furthermore, the same problem applies, and perhaps even more forcefully, to the normative aspect of the rules of recognition. Why, some commentators have asked, should judges and other legal officials be bound by the rules of recognition; what makes them obligatory in any sense? The problem is that though Hart nicely demonstrated the question, he has provided no answer; there is nothing in the practice theory of rules to explain why people would regard legal norms as binding, except pointing to the social fact that they do. Actually, Hart thought that this was enough; a philosophical account of the nature of law—as opposed to a normative, moral-political philosophy—can do no more than that. It can only point out that law has this normative element, and that wherever there is a functioning legal system in place, most members of the relevant population *regard* the requirements of law as binding—as giving them reasons for action and reasons for exerting pressure on other members to comply as well. Whether these reasons are moral reasons, and whether they are adequate to the task, are not questions that need to be answered within a general theory of jurisprudence.

I think that Hart is only partly correct about this issue. Consider the gunman situation again: The crucial difference between the gunman scenario and the law is much better explained by introducing the concept of authority. The gunman is only interested in getting your money. He does not claim—at least there is nothing in the situation to force him to claim—that he is in a position that authorizes him to order you to hand over your money. In other words, the gunman makes no claim to be a legitimate authority or to have a legitimate authoritative claim on your conduct. However, as Joseph Raz famously argued, it is an essential aspect of law that it always *claims* to be a legitimate authority.[28] When the law makes a claim to your money (by imposing a tax, or a fine, or whatever), it makes this claim as an exercise of its putative legitimate authority. And that is the sense in which legal requirements purport to create obligations; they are requirements based on claims of legitimate political authority. Needless to say, Raz does not suggest that law's claim to be a legitimate

[28] Raz, "Authority, Law, and Morality."

authority is generally a sound one, morally or otherwise justified. Whether the law's claim to the legitimacy of its authority is warranted or not—either in particular cases, or wholesale—is a separate, moral-political question, and the answers would vary from case to case. But it is essential to an understanding of what the law is, that it always makes this kind of claim—that it claims to be a legitimate political authority. What lessons can be drawn from Raz's insight, and how Hart's views need to be modified to accommodate those lessons, is the topic of our next chapter.

SUGGESTED FURTHER READINGS

Coleman, *Hart's Postscript: Essays on the Postscript to* The Concept of Law.
Dworkin, *Taking Rights Seriously.*
Gavison, *Issues in Contemporary Legal Philosophy: The Influence of H.L.A. Hart.*
MacCormick, *H.L.A. Hart.*

Authority, Conventions, and the Normativity of Law

IN THIS CHAPTER I would like to complete the outlines of a plausible version of legal positivism. The chapter is composed of two parts. In the first section I will discuss some of Joseph Raz's ideas about the nature of practical authority and the implications of his views about the normativity of law. In the second section I will return to the rules of recognition and try to show that, though H.L.A. Hart is basically right about the idea that social rules are at the foundations of law, we need a theory of social conventions to articulate the requisite foundations. With these two ideas in hand—the authoritative nature of law and its conventional foundations—we will have the main building blocks needed to reconstruct a plausible version of Hart's theory of law.

Raz's main insight, as noted in the previous chapter, is that the law necessarily claims to be a legitimate authority. There are three lessons I would like to draw from this general insight. First, though Hart is right that legal philosophy should confine itself to an explanation of the normativity of law—without slipping into a moral-political account of what makes law justified or worth having—we can still do better in explaining the normativity of law than just pointing out the fact that people tend to regard legal requirements as binding. As we will see in some detail below, Raz's account of practical authorities gives some structure to the normativity of law—explaining the kinds of reasons that would make legal instructions binding and their possible relation to moral and other normative considerations.

The second lesson I will draw from the authoritative nature of law is that legal norms are basically directives or instructions issued by an authority aiming to guide the conduct of others. In this respect, I will argue, legal norms are crucially different both from moral norms and from social norms. This will prove to be a controversial thesis, and part of its defense will be taken up only in the next chapter.

Finally, the third lesson is that, in spite of Hart's considerable efforts to detach an understanding of law from political sovereignty, these efforts went a bit too far. John Austin's command theory of law may have been too crude or too simplistic, but his basic insight—that law is an instrument of political sovereignty—is in the right direction. Raz's observation that law is essentially an authoritative institution holds these points together. It invites us to see that there is something unique to the normativity of law and in a way that ties law to political authority much more intimately than Hart's theory maintains. I will not propose any particular argument in support of this last point, but I hope that we will be able to see it as we go along.

Authority and Normativity

Whenever the law imposes an obligation or requires you to do something, it conveys a dual message: You *ought* to do it, and you ought to do it *because the law says so.* When the law prescribes a certain mode of conduct, it purports to make a practical difference that *it is the law* that requires it. If you recall the California signposts about the hands-free mobile phone requirement, the signposts got it exactly right: We ought to use a hands-free device, they remind us, *because* "it's the law!" This is one of the crucial respects in which both moral requirements and social norms are different from law. When you are presented with a moral reason for action that applies to you under the circumstances, or are told that there is a social norm that requires you to do something (say, greet an acquaintance or bring a bottle of wine to the dinner party), it would be rather silly and pointless if you ask, "Who says so?" Nobody does, of course; it is not a relevant question. But in the legal case, it always is. It always matters that it is the law (or some particular legal authority) that says so. One of the 61 main challenges about the explanation of the normativity of law is precisely to explain this connection between reasons for action and the relevance of the answer to the "who says so?" question. So let us begin with some general observations about these types of reasons for action, and then see how Raz's theory of authority explains this crucial aspect of the normativity of law.

There are several types of cases in which a person may have a reason to do something because she was told by somebody to do it. Sometimes, of course, one has a reason to do what the other recommends or suggests simply because the recommendation is sound on its merits. When I ask my daughter to finish her homework before she goes out to meet with her friends, I expect her to comply with the request because I believe that she has a reason to finish her homework regardless of my asking her to do so. The purpose of my request is simply to remind her of something that she has a reason to do independently of my request. However, if I ask a friend to help me with moving a heavy piece of furniture, I expect the friend to comply with my request, in crucial part because it is my request. I am not suggesting that the friend would have an independent reason to move the furniture whether I ask him to do so or not. Let me call these latter kinds of reasons *identity related*. Somewhat loosely expressed, these would be the kinds of reasons where A's reason to φ partly depends on the identity of another agent, B, who suggests, requests, or orders A to $\underline{\varphi}$.[1]

There are various situations in which a reason for action is identity related. Some of them pertain to knowledge. Suppose that my broker (if I had one) recommends that I sell my shares in GM because she predicts that their value will plummet. Being ignorant about such matters, as I am, I have a pretty good reason to do what the broker recommends. And the fact that it is my broker who recommends this course of action and not, say, my department chair, is crucially relevant (for example, when asked by

---

[1] In the literature, these reasons are often called *content-independent reasons*; I find this expression somewhat confusing (because the reasons are not entirely content independent, only partly), and hence allowed myself to introduce the notion of identity-related reasons.

somebody why did I sell my shares, it would make perfect sense to reply that I did so because my broker had recommended that I do so). The assumption is that she just knows better what reasons apply to me and that, by following her recommendation, I am more likely to comply with the reasons that apply to me than by trying to figure it out by myself.

In other cases, however, the reason to do what another person tells you to do has nothing to do with knowledge or expertise. The example of complying with a request of a friend is one such case. The connection is not epistemic; it is not the case that your reason to comply with a request of a friend has anything to do with the fact that the friend knows better what reasons apply to you. The fact that it is your friend who asked you to help constitutes part of the reason to do what he asked because he is your friend, and because the value of friendship is such that there are good reasons to abide by friends' requests.

The law essentially purports to generate identity-related reasons for action. When the law prescribes a certain mode of conduct, it purports to make a practical difference that *it is the law* that requires it. Therefore, it is one of the main questions about the normativity of law: how to explain the rationale of identity-related reasons of the kind the law purports to generate. I think that Joseph Raz has suggested the most plausible answer: The law is essentially an authoritative institution and the reasons to comply with an authoritative directive are, by their very nature, identity-related reasons.

The main challenge facing any explanation of the nature of authority is to make sense of the idea that a person may have an obligation to do something because another person has instructed her to do it. I use the word *obligation* advisedly. There are many situations in which identity-related reasons for action make perfect sense in contexts that have nothing to do with authority. Complying with a request of a friend or acting on the advice of an expert are examples already mentioned. What makes authoritative instructions unique is not that they generate identity-related reasons, though they necessarily do that as well, but the fact that those reasons are of an obligatory nature. If *A* has legitimate authority over *B* in context *C*, then *A*'s authoritative

63

directive requiring B to φ in C would normally entail that B has an obligation to φ.[2]

Raz's main insight is that the way to justify an obligation to follow an authority's directive is by showing that there are cases in which a person is systematically more likely to comply with obligations[3] that apply to him if he follows the authority's instruction than by trying to figure out (or, act on) those obligations by himself. In other words, an authority is legitimate when it provides a service—the service of making it more likely that, in the relevant area of its authority, the subject would act as he or she *ought* to act if he or she follows the authority's instructions rather than trying to act without the authoritative guidance. Raz calls this the normal justification thesis:

> the normal way to establish that a person has authority over another person involves showing that the alleged subject is likely better to comply with reasons that apply to him . . . if he accepts the directives of the alleged authority as authoritatively binding and tries to follow them, rather than by trying to follow the reasons which apply to him directly.[4]

Admittedly, the details of Raz's account are controversial. In particular, Raz's formulations make it somewhat unclear how his account allows us to distinguish between cases in which reasons for action are identity related, as in the case of following an expert's advice, and genuine authoritative relations, where the authority's instruction constitutes not just identity-related reasons but also an obligation to comply. Furthermore, if we cannot explain how an authoritative directive generates an obligation to comply, we would also lack an account of what gives a putative authority the right to issue such directives—we would lack an account of what gives anyone a right to rule.[5]

---

[2] *Pro tanto* obligation, not absolute and not all things considered.

[3] Raz uses the word "reasons" in his formulation, not obligations, and he may not agree with my suggested modifications here.

[4] Raz, *The Morality of Freedom*, 53.

[5] Both of these objections have been forcefully advanced by Stephen Darwall, "Authority and Second-Personal Reasons for Acting." In a recent (yet unpublished) article, "The Role of Authority," Scott Hershovitz further develops these

My own view is that Raz's theory makes more sense if the normal justification thesis is confined to facilitating the obligations that apply to the authority's putative subjects; the only way to get the conclusion that there is an obligation to follow the directive of a legitimate authority is to assume that the role of a practical authority is to make it more likely that its subjects would comply better with the obligations that apply to them by following the authority's directive than by trying to figure it out for themselves. Needless to say, this view depends on the availability of a fairly robust distinction between reasons for action and a particular subset of such reasons that constitute an obligation or duty. I am not assuming that we have a very satisfactory account of the distinction; but we should, because it is very intuitive. The idea is that there are countless things we may have a reason to do, but only some of them we also have an obligation to do. Note, however, that if you are doubtful about the availability of such a distinction then you need not worry about Raz's account either. In that case, you will be forced to admit that it does not matter whether an authoritative directive constitutes an obligation or only a reason to comply.

Admittedly, even if we confine the legitimacy conditions of authority to cases in which following its directives makes it more likely that we will comply with obligations that apply to us, we may still lack an account of what gives any putative authority a right to issue such directives, that is, we would still lack a general framework of the idea of the right to rule.[6] I do not find this to be a weakness of Raz's theory; on the contrary, it seems to me much more plausible to maintain that nobody has a right to rule, not even a legitimate authority. Telling other people what to do may be justified under countless circumstances, but I doubt that

---

critical themes. For my own stab at some of these vexing issues, see my "The Dilemma of Authority" (draft posted on the Social Science Research Network, www.ssrn.com).

[6] Darwall ("Authority and Second-Personal Reasons for Acting") gives a nice example: Even if A is morally obliged to invest the family savings according to expert advice, it does not follow that the expert gains an authority to guide A's investments.

it is something that anyone can acquire as a matter of right.[7] (It is possible that particular persons or institutions may have a right to occupy a certain authoritative role, but that is a different matter and one that is typically justified on procedural grounds.) In any case, these details, important as they may be, do not matter for our purposes here, that is, as long as we would concede that the service conception of practical authorities, the basic idea of the normal justification thesis, forms at least a necessary—though perhaps not sufficient—condition for the legitimacy of a practical authority. What we need to explain in the legal context is the rationale of the kinds of normative demands that the law purports to make—that you ought to do X and that you ought to do it partly because the law says so.

The first part—that you ought to do X—is explained by the idea that the function of authorities is to facilitate our ability to act on the reasons that apply to us anyway, that is, regardless of authorities. The second, identity-related part—that you ought to do X because the law says so—is explained by the service conception, or rationale, of practical authorities. The assumption has to be that the authority is somehow in a position to make it more likely that you will comply with what you ought to do by following its directives than by trying to figure it out for yourself. Even if these two conditions are not quite sufficient to explain the range of issues that any theory of practical authority would have to explain, at least they provide the core idea of what would make compliance with a legal directive rational and obligatory.[8]

---

[7] For a more detailed argument to that effect, see Arneson, "Democracy Is Not Intrinsically Just."

[8] Let me try to clarify a terminological point here: The word "ought" is sometimes used interchangeably with the word "obligation" or "duty." Generally, however, "ought" has a broader and looser use. For example, we often use the word "ought" as an indication of an all-things-considered reason, as in, for example, "I ought to finish this article." The word "obligation" or "duty," however, stands for a much more structured and narrower concept. To say that "I have an obligation to finish the paper" would imply that I have a reason to do it, and one that is structured in a certain way; it is a reason to finish the paper and a reason to exclude certain types of considerations to count against this reason, etc. A full account of the nature of obligations cannot be given here. See, e.g., Raz, *Practical Reason and Norms*.

If this general idea is correct, some important implications follow about the nature of law and its normative character. First, the authoritative nature of law gives considerable support to the idea that legal norms are basically instructions issued by some persons in order to guide the conduct of others. This is a very controversial idea. The objection to it is that norms can be legally valid even if they do not originate with any particular authority. There are two main versions of this argument. One argument, alluded to by Hart in the context of his critique of Austin, concerns the prevalence of legal constraints on authorities. The second argument pertains to the general claim that sometimes we can deduce the content of the law by way of reasoning or moral justification. This latter objection is rather complex and I will leave it for the next chapter, where I will discuss it in some detail. For now, let me answer the first objection.

One of the difficulties Hart raised about Austin's command theory of law concerns the legal constraints on lawmaking authority. If the law simply is the command of the sovereign, how can we explain the fact that, in countless jurisdictions, the sovereign is bound by law. There are constitutional and other legal constraints that curtail the sovereign's authority to make laws of certain kinds or in certain ways. If there are legal constraints on lawmaking authority, how can we say that all law originates with such authorities?

The underlying point of this argument seems to be that an authority cannot be self-binding in the requisite sense. I doubt, however, that the idea of self-binding authority is an absurd one. To begin with, authorities, just like ordinary persons, can make decisions that are binding themselves.[9] The making of a promise (as Hart himself mentions) would be a paradigmatic example. A person who expresses a promise thus undertakes a commitment—one that binds her and constraints her future reasons for action.[10]

---

[9] The idea is familiar from the literature on precommitment. See, e.g., Elster, *Ulysses Unbound*.

[10] I suspect that Hart failed to see the point here, in spite of his own reference to the promise example, because he must have subscribed to the so-called practice theory of promises, whereby promises only work on the basis of some

But one may still wonder whether Raz's service conception of authority is compatible with an idea of a self-binding authoritative decision. Remember that the idea is that the whole point of an authority is to facilitate better compliance with reasons for action. The assumption has to be that an authority's subject is more likely to comply with the reasons that apply to her if she follows the authority's directive than if she tries to figure out or act on those reasons by herself. How can this rationale apply to the authority itself? In other words, authorities generate identity-related reasons for action; but it seems that identity-related reasons cannot apply to the same agent whose identity is relevant to the reasons generated.

Actually, I think that this objection holds only with respect to the cases in which identity-related reasons rest on expertise. My (imagined) broker is an expert relative to me, for example, and therefore I have reasons to take her advice very seriously; but surely she is not an expert relative to herself. In this sense, it makes no sense indeed to say that a person is an authority vis-à-vis herself. But not all cases involve such epistemic considerations. To take a simple example: Suppose that there is a recurring coordination problem, say in circumstances C, that needs to be solved (that is, suppose we *ought* to solve it). Suppose, further, that no solution is likely to emerge naturally, so to speak, unless someone makes a decision and communicates it to the parties concerned. Now, you—one of the parties concerned—happen to be in a position that enables you to make the decision and communicate it to the others: "In circumstances C we do X"; and then, if everybody complies, the coordination problem is solved. This could be an example of a self-binding authority. You have made an authoritative decision that binds you in exactly the same way, and for the same reasons, that it binds the others. There is nothing inherently absurd about the idea that an authority may issue

conventional practice of promising that prevails in society. I think that Hart assumed that there must be some rules about promising in the background before any speech act of promising can gain the significance that it has. But the practice conception of promising is far from obvious and has been quite convincingly rejected by some philosophers (e.g., Scanlon in his *What We Owe to Each Other*, chap. 7). I have explained some of this in my *Social Conventions*, chap. 5.

directives that bind the authority itself. Under certain conditions, authorities can be self-binding.

I am not suggesting that this is the main rationale of most prevalent legal constraints on lawmaking authorities. The most common constraints on lawmaking authority are constitutional. In most legal systems these days, a written constitution defines the lawmaking authority of various institutions and establishes certain mechanisms for adjudicating potentially controversial cases about such matters. Nothing in the nature of constitutions poses a challenge to Raz's thesis. Constitutions are authoritative directives determining the legal powers of various institutions and often imposing various legal constraints on the exercise of those powers. There is nothing problematic in the idea that one authority can bind or constrain the power of another.

Let me conclude: The fact that lawmaking authority is often legally constrained does not, by itself, count against the thesis that law essentially consists of authoritative directives or instructions. If there is a serious challenge to this thesis, it comes from a different direction; the challenge is posed by those who argue that norms can be legally valid by reasoning about what the law ought to be. I will discuss this challenge at length in the next chapter.

Before we proceed, let me deal with this nagging doubt about our underlying assumption here: What if the law is not more than an organized group of gunmen? Could it not be the case that Austin was right, and the difference between the law and the gunmen is only a matter of scope? One gunman does not make law; but a whole bunch of them, acting in some organized fashion and sustaining control over a certain population, could well be law. Why not? And, if so, just like the gunmen who need not make a claim to be a legitimate authority, perhaps the law need not make such a claim either? It could be argued that Raz's insight that the law claims to be a legitimate authority does not necessarily hold true.[11] Perhaps it is true in most civilized societies, not because

[11] Note, however, that historical examples would not settle this question. Even the most draconian terror regimes that we know from history do not necessarily undermine Raz's argument that the law *claims* legitimate authority. Those horrible regimes and the agents who acted on their behalf tended to claim legitimacy, incredible and outrageous as such claims were. Furthermore, it is worth keeping

it is law, but because they are civilized societies in which governance is generally regarded as requiring moral legitimacy. So the question is, why would a gunmen-type control over a given population not be law?

Note that there are, actually, two different questions here. First, there is the age-old question of whether a regime of sheer terror that has no plausible claim to legitimacy can possibly count as law, or not. I will not purport to provide an answer to this question, mostly because I believe that it is not theoretically important to give one. Some forms of social control might be borderline cases of law. Certain regimes might have some features that would make them legal, and others that would not. Borderline cases are just that, borderline cases. The second and more important question is whether there is something about the nature of law itself that requires it to make a claim to be a legitimate authority. And here I think that Raz's positive answer is correct. As I understand the answer, it consists of two points. The first is that whenever the law makes a certain requirement about the conduct of its putative subjects, it purports to impose the requirement as a matter of obligation or duty to comply; it is the way in which laws are invariably expressed. The second is that the only way to make sense of this kind of obligation is by interpreting it as an instance of an authoritative directive. And here the basic insight is the same as the one noted by Hart: If I tell you that you ought to φ, I have appealed to reasons that apply to you; if I tell you that you should φ *only* because otherwise I will harm you, I have renounced a claim to reasons that apply to you—except the reason to avoid the harm that I might inflict on you. Therefore, whenever the law expresses a demand in terms of what its putative subjects *ought* to do, as the law invariably does, it appeals to reasons, albeit of the identity-related kind. And the best way to make sense of such identity-related reasons in the context of law is by interpreting them as authoritative in nature. (Remember that law's essential

---

in mind that in any functioning legal system, morally wicked as it may be, the law fulfills some functions that may be quite valuable regardless of the overall iniquity of the regime. And if it does not even do that, then it may be questionable that there is law in that society. It may be a borderline case of law or not law at all.

claim to the legitimacy of its authority can always fail to be true or justified, either wholesale, or in any given case.)

So now we can move to the second lesson I would like to draw from the authoritative nature of law, and it concerns law's normative character. Raz's thesis about the essentially authoritative nature of law gives us the basic structure of the kinds of reasons we may have for regarding the law as binding. It explains the sense in which a legal obligation can be an obligation to do something because the law says so. Raz's account, however, does more than that: It resolves an important aspect of the debate between Hart and Kelsen about the relations between legal obligations and moral ones. According to Kelsen, as noted in chapter 1, the difference between a moral ought and a legal ought is not a difference in the relevant nature of "ought," but only a difference in point of view. Hart's account of the normativity of law, as we saw in the previous chapter, is entirely reductive. It purports to explain the normativity of law in sociological terms, given by the details of the practice theory of rules. This reductionism leads Hart to the conclusion that legal obligations, and other normative aspects of law, can be explained without any reference to morality or moral reasons for action. Whether in any given case there is a moral reason to abide by a legal obligations is, for Hart, purely a moral question that has nothing to do with the nature of legal "ought." When we talk about a legal obligation, we basically describe a complex social reality. When we talk about a moral obligation, we express a judgment about the way things ought to be. Thus, somewhat crudely, Hart would say that, in the moral context, it makes perfect sense to distinguish between what people (in any given population) *believe* that ought to be done, and what ought to be done. In the legal context, if the relevant population believes that there is a legal obligation to φ, then ipso facto, there is such a legal obligation.[12]

You might suspect that this is just another way of expressing the question about the possibility of reduction: Hart maintains that the normative language of the law is reducible to social facts

---

[12] This is somewhat crude since, even in the legal context, we must make room for the possibility that anyone, including judges, can make a mistake about the law. I will discuss this problem in the next chapter.

(about people's beliefs and attitudes), whereas Kelsen seems to deny the possibility of such a reduction. To some extent, this is true. But let me suggest that Raz's thesis about the authoritative nature of law shows that both Hart and Kelsen have missed something important. Even if Hart is right that legal ought is reducible to facts about people's beliefs and attitudes, one would still have to give an account of what it is that people need to believe in order to make sense of attributing an "ought" to the content of a legal directive.

The point is that the idea of practical authority gives some structure to the rationality of such beliefs. Raz's thesis does not come in to settle the question about reductionism, at least not directly. What it shows is that the way in which we can make sense of a legal ought, or the way in which law is regarded as binding—normatively speaking—is by way of understanding the role of law as an authoritative resolution. The general conditions of an authority's legitimacy provide the framework for connecting a legal ought to a moral ought. The law is morally obligatory if its claim to legitimate authority is morally warranted.[13] At the same time, Raz's thesis proves Kelsen to be wrong as well. Legal ought is not, as Kelsen maintained, just like a moral ought from a different point of view. On the one hand, there is nothing in the structure of morality that connects an "ought" to authority or, in fact, to identity-related reasons. Legal ought, on the other hand, is essentially identity related, because it is authoritative. Furthermore, you may recall that I have complained about Kelsen's account of the normativity of law, that it leaves the choice of adopting any given basic norm to be entirely whimsical, devoid of an explanation of the kinds of reasons people may have for endorsing the basic norm. But now we can see that there are such reasons: the reasons for acknowledging the legitimacy of the relevant legal authority. If, and to the extent that, a legal authority fulfills the conditions of legitimacy, one would have a reason to regard law's

---

[13] I am not saying if and *only if*. There may be all sorts of moral reasons to comply with the law even if the law fails the conditions of legitimate authority. In other words, an obligation to obey the law may be present even if the law fails in its claim to legitimacy. This point is widely recognized in the literature on political obligation.

instructions or directives as morally binding (*pro tanto*, of course, and not necessarily all things considered).

Where does it leave the question about the possibility of reduction? I think that Raz's thesis about the authoritative nature of law leaves Hart's reductionist framework intact. The requirements of law, whether obligations or other normative prescriptions, are authoritative resolutions. Now, of course, whether a directive has actually been issued by an authority or not is a question of fact—a non-normative fact, that is. Therefore, as long as we can show that (1) law always consists of authoritative directives and (2) the question of who counts as a legal authority and how such authority is to be exercised is determined by social rules, we have laid the foundations for a reduction of legality to facts of a non-normative kind. Further considerations that support (1) will be discussed in the next chapter. Here I want to discuss the considerations that support (2).

THE CONVENTIONAL FOUNDATIONS OF LAW

Let us assume that legal norms consist of authoritative instructions or directives. What we need, therefore, is an account of who counts as a *legal* authority in any given legal system. Hart's idea about the rules of recognition would seem to provide a very plausible answer: In each and every society that has a functioning legal system, there are certain social rules followed by the relevant population that determine who counts as the legal authority and how such authority is structured.

However, it turns out that a satisfactory account of the nature of these social rules of recognition, and the ways in which they might constitute the idea of legality, proves to be rather elusive. Some commentators have noted that there is really nothing in Hart's practice theory of the rules of recognition that would explain why people, mostly judges and other officials, are bound to follow those rules. What makes it the case that judges are obliged to follow the rules of recognition? Pointing to the fact that judges take themselves to be bound by those rules does not quite answer the question. What makes it rational for them to do so?

Some years after *The Concept of Law* was published, the philosopher David Lewis came up with a very sophisticated account of social conventions.[14] Lewis was mostly interested in the nature of language, but he offered an ingenious general theory about conventional norms. The basic idea is that conventions are normative solutions to recurrent large-scale coordination problems. A coordination problem arises when several agents have a particular structure of preferences with respect to their mutual modes of conduct—that between several alternatives of conduct open to them in a given set of circumstances, each and every agent has a stronger preference to act in concert with the other agents than his own preference for acting upon any one of the particular alternatives. Most coordination problems in our lives are easily solved by simple agreements between the agents to act upon one, more or less arbitrarily chosen, alternative, thus securing concerted action among them. However, when a particular coordination problem is recurrent in a given set of circumstances—and agreement is difficult to obtain (mostly because of the large number of agents involved)—a social rule is very likely to emerge, and this rule is a convention. Conventions emerge as solutions to large-scale recurrent coordination problems—not as a result of an agreement, but as an alternative to such an agreement, precisely in those cases where agreements are difficult or impossible to obtain.

When this novel account of conventions came to be known, some legal philosophers realized that it may provide the explanation of the nature of the rules of recognition. If the rules of recognition are social conventions, we would have in Lewis's theory both an account of how such rules emerge (like any other convention) and the rationale of following them (to solve large-scale recurrent coordination problems). Thus a conventionalist account of the rules of recognition has emerged, and one that Hart himself, years later, seemed to endorse in his postscript to *The Concept of Law*. As he put it, the rule of recognition "is in effect a form of judicial customary rule existing only if it is accepted and practiced in the law-identifying and law-applying operations of the courts."

[14] See Lewis, *Convention: A Philosophical Study*.

And he added: "certainly the rule of recognition is treated in my book as resting on a conventional form of judicial consensus."[15]

Many contemporary philosophers of law, however, think that this conventionalist turn about the nature of the rules of recognition was a turn for the worse. Ronald Dworkin, for one, argues that there are no rules of recognition at all. Others, more sympathetic to Hart's legal positivist conception of law, argue that a conventionalist understanding of the rules of recognition is fraught with difficulties, and that such a view generates more problems than it solves. To the contrary, I will argue here that with some important modifications the conventionalist account of the rules of recognition is sound.

Before I try to explain the modifications we need, let me say a few words in response to the more fundamental objection to Hart's account, raised by Dworkin. Dworkin denies that the criteria employed by judges and other officials in determining what counts as law are determined by rules, and thus he denies that there are any rules of recognition at all. But as far as I can see, Dworkin's argument is based on a single observation, which is rather implausible. He argues that it cannot be the case that, in identifying the law, judges follow rules, because judges often disagree about the criteria of legality in their legal systems, so much so that it makes no sense to suggest that there are any rules of recognition at all, or else, the rules become so abstract that it becomes pointless to insist that they are rules.[16]

The problem is this: To show that there are no rules of recognition, Dworkin would have had to show that the disagreements judges have about the criteria of legality in their jurisdictions are not just in the margins, that they go all the way down to the core. But this is just not plausible. Could we have anyone in a judicial role in the United States, for example, who seriously doubts that

---

[15] Hart, postscript to *The Concept of Law* (henceforth Postscript), 256–66.

[16] Dworkin, *Law's Empire*, chap. 1. The same idea is reiterated in Dworkin's recent book, *Justice in Robes*, 164, 190–96. This should not be confused with a different and much more interesting claim that Dworkin also makes: Even if there are rules of recognition, they do not settle the question of legal validity. Norms can be legally valid, Dworkin argues, even if they do not derive their validity from the rules of recognition. This argument will be discussed in the next chapter.

acts of Congress make law? Or that the U.S. Constitution prevails over other forms of legislation? More importantly, as mentioned several times before,[17] there is an inherent limit to how much disagreement about criteria of legality it makes sense to attribute to judges, because the judges' role as institutional players is constituted by those same rules that they allegedly disagree about. The role and authority of certain persons qua judges are constituted by the rules of recognition. Before judges can come to disagree about any legal issue, they must first be able to see themselves as *institutional* players, playing, as it were, a fairly structured role in an elaborate practice. Judges can only see themselves as such on the basis of the rules and conventions that establish their role and authority as judges. In short, pointing to the fact that judges often have certain disagreements about the content of the rules of recognition simply cannot prove that there are no such rules. On the contrary, we can only make sense of such disagreements on the basis of the assumption that there are rules of recognition that constitute, inter alia, the courts system and the legal authority of judges.

So let us make the plausible assumption that there are some rules, mostly followed by judges and other legal officials, determining who counts as a legal authority in the relevant legal system. Are these rules conventions? If we think that the only rationale of social conventions consists in normative solutions to large-scale coordination problems, as Lewis suggested, then the answer is probably no. But let me suggest a more general characterization of conventions that does not tie the function or rationale of conventions to the solution of coordination problems.

Two main features are intuitively associated with conventional rules. First, conventional rules are, in a specific sense, *arbitrary*. Roughly, if a rule is a convention, we should be able to point to an alternative rule that we could have followed instead, achieving basically the same purpose. Second, conventional rules normally lose their point if they are not *actually followed* in the relevant community. The reasons for following a rule that is conventional depend on the fact that others (in the relevant population) follow

[17] Hart, *The Concept of Law*, 133.

it, too. To give one familiar example, consider the almost universal convention of saying the word "hello" when responding to a telephone call. Both features are clearly manifest in this example. Presumably, there is some purpose or point in having a recognizable expression that would indicate to the caller that one has picked up the phone. But, of course, using the particular expression "hello" is quite arbitrary; any other, similar expression would have served us just as well—as long as the expression we use is one that others use, too. If the point of the convention is to have an expression that can be easily and quickly recognized, then people would have a reason to follow the norm—use the expression that others in the community follow as well. And if, for some reason, most people no longer use this expression (as seems to be the case these days), one would no longer have any particular reason to use it either.

Both of these intuitive features of conventional norms can be captured by the following definition:

A rule, R, is conventional if and only if all the following conditions obtain:

(1) There is a group of people, a population, P, that normally follows R in circumstances C.

(2) There is a reason, or a combination of reasons—call it A—for members of P to follow R in circumstances C.

(3) There is at least one other potential rule, S, that if members of P had actually followed in circumstances C, then A would have been a sufficient reason for members of P to follow S instead of R in circumstances C, and at least partly because S is the rule generally followed instead of R.

The rules R and S are such that it is impossible (or pointless) to comply with both of them concomitantly in circumstances C.[18]

As we just saw, Dworkin's objection to the rules of recognition denies the truth of premise (1). But we also saw that this objection fails, so let us assume that (1) is true. Given the truth of (1), it

---

[18] I suggested this definition and elaborated on it in much greater detail in my *Social Conventions*, chap. 1.

would be extremely unlikely that (2) is false. If judges and other officials follow certain rules that determine what law is, surely they follow them for reasons. What those reasons, generally speaking are, however, turns out to be somewhat difficult to answer. In his original account of the rules of recognition, Hart suggested that the rationale of the rules of recognition consists in the need for certainty. In a developed legal system, Hart argued, people would need to be able *to identify* what types of norms are legally valid. In fact, he presented this advantage of the rules of recognition in providing certainty about the valid sources of law as the main distinguishing factor between "primitive," prelegal normative systems and a developed legal order.[19] Later, in his postscript to *The Concept of Law*, Hart seems to have added another kind of reason for having rules of recognition, basically of a coordinative nature:

> Certainly the rule of recognition is treated in my book as resting on a conventional form of judicial custom. That it does so rest seems quite clear at least in English and American law for surely an English judge's reason for treating Parliament's legislation (or an American judges' reason for treating the Constitution) as a source of law having supremacy over other sources includes the fact that his judicial colleagues concur in this as their predecessors have done.[20]

I have some doubts about both of these explanations. That the rules of recognition contribute to our certainty about what counts as law in our society is surely true. But is it the main reason for having such rules? This I doubt. It is like suggesting that there are some rules or conventions about what constitutes a theater performance so as to enable us to identify this form of art as distinguished from other, similar artistic endeavors. Surely, if there are some conventions that constitute what theater is, it is because there are some artistic reasons for having this form of art in the first place. Similarly, I would suggest, if there are reasons to have rules of recognition, those reasons must be very intimately linked to the reasons for having law and the main functions of law in

---

[19] Hart, *The Concept of Law*, chap. 5.

[20] Postscript, 267.

society. Certainty about what law is cannot be the main reason for having law. There must be some reasons for having law first, and then it might also be important to have a certain level of certainty about it. It cannot be the other way around. I am not suggesting that the reasons for having rules of recognition are the same as the reasons for having law in a society. My claim is that the reasons for having rules of recognition are closely tied to those reasons and, in some ways (yet to be specified), they instantiate them.

The coordinative rationale of the rules of recognition is even more suspect, and for reasons that are quite explicit in Hart's writings. It is true that judges and other legal agents, acting in their official capacities, need a great deal of coordination in various respects. In particular, they would need to follow basically those same rules that other officials in their legal system follow in identifying the relevant sources of law in their legal system. That the rules of recognition enable this kind of coordination in the various actions of legal officials is not disputable. But again, it makes little sense to suggest that this is the main rationale of the rules of recognition. As mentioned above, for judges to have any coordination problem that might need a solution, first we must be able to identify them *as judges*; we first need a set of rules that constitutes their specific institutional roles. In short, and more generally, first we need the institutions of law; then we may also have some coordination problems that may require a normative solution. The basic role of the rules of recognition is to constitute the relevant institutions. The fundamental rules of recognition of a legal system are constitutive rules (or conventions, as we shall see), and their coordination functions are secondary at best.

There is a rather striking confusion in some of the literature on the conventionality of the rules of recognition that connects these two points. Because the standard understanding of conventions has been the one offered by Lewis, which consists of the idea that conventions are normative solutions to coordination problems, commentators have been drawn to the idea that, if the rules of recognition are conventions, their basic rationale must be a coordinative one. But commentators have also realized that the rationale of the rules of recognition must be closely tied to the reasons for having law in the first place. And the combination of these two points has led many to assume that the main rationale *of law itself*—the main reasons for having law in society—is also coordinative in nature.[21] This has rendered legal conventionalism, as this view came to be called, rather implausible. The idea that law's main functions in society can be reduced to the solution of coordination problems is all too easy to refute. Solving coordination problems, as complex and intricate as they may be, is only one of the main functions of law in society, and probably not the most important one.[22]

I mention this confusion partly because Leslie Green's critique of legal conventionalism, often cited as a main argument against a conventionalist construal of the rules of recognition, is based on it. Green is absolutely right to claim that the authority of law, and its main moral-political rationale, cannot be explained in terms of law's function in solving coordination problems.[23] But he is wrong to conclude that this undermines a conventionalist account of the rules of recognition. Neither the main functions of law in society nor the main rationale of the rules of recognition have much to do with solving coordination problems.

We have yet to show that the rules of recognition are conventions. The conventionality of the rules of recognition crucially depends on the third condition—on the question of whether the rules are arbitrary and compliance dependent in the requisite sense. So let us turn to examine this aspect of the rules of recognition. On the face of it, the arbitrariness of the rules of recognition is strongly supported by the following two observations. First, we know that different legal systems, even ones that are very similar in many other respects, have different rules of recognition. The rules followed in the United States in recognizing the sources of American law are very different from those followed, for instance, in the United Kingdom about the recognition of British

---

[21] See, e.g., Lagerspetz, *The Opposite Mirrors*, and Hartogh, *Mutual Expectations: A Conventionalist Theory of Law*. Dworkin's interpretation of what he calls *legal conventionalism* relies on a very similar idea. See his *Law's Empire*, chap. 7.

[22] Notice that coordination problems are much easier to solve than the other types of collective-action problems because there is no serious conflict of interest between the parties involved.

[23] See Green's "Positivism and Conventionalism," 43–49.

law. Second, there is a very clear sense in which the reasons for following the rules of recognition are compliance dependent in the relevant sense. This is one of the points that Hart has rightly emphasized in his postscript to *The Concept of Law*—that the reasons judges and other officials have for following certain norms about the identification of the sources of law in their legal systems are closely tied to the fact that other officials follow those same norms.

I do not think that either of these observations supporting the conventionality of the rules of recognition is really controversial. The reasons critics have for doubting the conventionality of the rules of recognition pertain to the normative aspect of the rules. Again, Green was one of those who observed this difficulty in the conventional account of the rule of recognition. As he put it, "Hart's view that the fundamental rules [of recognition] are 'mere conventions' continues to sit uneasily with any notion of obligation," and thus, with the intuition that the rules of recognition point to the sources of law that "judges are legally bound to apply."[24] So the problem seems to be this: If the rules of recognition are *arbitrary* in the requisite sense, how can we explain the fact that they are supposed to obligate judges and other legal officials to follow them?

I think that by now we have all the tools we need to answer this question. First, even if Green had been right to assume that the main conventionalist rationale of the rules of recognition is a coordinative one, the puzzle he raises about their potential normativity is easily answered. Some coordination problems are such that there is an obligation to solve them. If a conventional solution has emerged, the relevant agents may well have an obligation to follow the conventional solution. However, since I do not think that the rules of recognition are coordination conventions, I will not avail myself to this simple answer. The main answer to Green's puzzle resides in the distinction between the idea of a legal obligation to follow the rules of recognition and the separate moral or political question of whether judges (or anyone else for that matter) have reasons to engage in the practice that is constituted by those rules.

The rules of recognition, like the rules of chess, determine what the practice is. They constitute the rules of the game, so to speak. Like other constitutive rules, they have a dual function: They determine what constitutes the practice and prescribe modes of conduct within it. The *legal* obligation to follow the rules of recognition is just like the chess player's obligation to, say, move the bishop—if one is to move it—only diagonally. Both are prescribed by the rules of the game. What such rules cannot prescribe, however, is an "ought" about playing the game to begin with. Conventional practices create reasons for action only if the relevant agent has a reason to participate in the practice to begin with. And that is true of the law as well. If there is an "ought" to play the game, so to speak, then this "ought" cannot be expected to come from the rules of recognition. The obligation to play by the rules—to follow the law, if there is one—must come from moral and political considerations. The reasons for obeying the law cannot be derived from the norms that determine what the law is.

Thus, my main response to Green's worries about the normativity of the rules of recognition is this: Once we realize that the rules of recognition are constitutive and not coordinative conventions, we can see that there is really nothing unique or particularly puzzling about the idea that judges ought to follow the rules. The sense in which a judge is obliged to follow the rules of recognition is exactly like the obligation of an umpire in a cricket game to follow the rules of cricket. Both obligations are conditional. If, and to the extent that the judge or the umpire have reasons to play the game, the rules simply determine what their obligations in the game are; they constitute what the game is. In both cases, however, we cannot expect the rules of the game to constitute the reason to play it. In other words, the internal (legal) obligation is determined by the rules themselves; the rules that constitute the game also prescribe modes of conduct within it. The external obligation (or, generally, reasons) to play the game, if there is one, is a different matter—one that cannot be expected to be determined on the basis of the normativity of the rules of the game. Whether judges, or anybody else, would have an obligation to play the game, as it were, is always a separate question—one that needs to be determined on moral-political grounds.

Let me summarize some conclusions. Hart's reductionist project relies on the idea that the conditions of legal validity are determined by the social rules of recognition. I argued here that a plausible conventionalist construal of this thesis is available. However, I also argued that Hart's reductionism about the normativity of law is overly simplistic and needs to be modified by Raz's important insight that law always claims to be a legitimate authority. The authoritative nature of law, I suggested, supports the construal of legal norms as instructions or directives issued by legal authorities. These two points, taken together, would entail the following two theses:

(1) In every society that has a functioning legal system, there are some social conventions that determine who counts as legal authority in that society and how its authority is to be exercised.

(2) Legal norms consist of the directives or instructions of legal authorities—those authorities that are identified and constituted by the social conventions of (1).

This, I believe, is a somewhat modified version of Hart's version of legal positivism. In the next two chapters we will consider some important challenges that have been leveled at these ideas, and we will try to assess their force. The next chapter is devoted to a detailed defense of the second thesis.

Suggested Further Readings

Green, *The Authority of the State.*
Marmor, *Social Conventions: From Language to Law.*
Raz, *Between Authority and Interpretation.*
———, *The Morality of Freedom*, chaps. 1–4, 7.
Shapiro, "Authority," 382.

Is Law Determined by Morality?

THE IDEA THAT the law consists of authoritative directives has been met with considerable skepticism over the last few decades. Many legal philosophers have argued that the overall content of the law is much more diverse than content that is communicated by legal authorities. In particular, it has been argued that moral considerations can sometimes determine what the law is. The content of the law, according to these views, is partly deduced by moral (and perhaps other types of evaluative) reasoning. So this is the challenge I want to consider in this chapter. We will take a closer look at some of the main arguments purporting to demonstrate that law cannot be separated from morality. I will try to show that there are several important insights that these arguments illuminate, but that eventually they fail to prove that legal content depends on moral truths.

JUDICIAL DISCRETION AND LEGAL PRINCIPLES

H.L.A. Hart clearly recognized that his views about the nature of law entail that the law is bound to run out. It is inevitable, he argued, that cases would come before courts of law that are not settled by the existing law. Law is a finite set of rules and directives, and those rules cannot possibly determine an outcome about every possible case that would need some legal resolution. Since judges rarely have the option of not deciding a legal case they adjudicate, it is inevitable that some cases that they have to decide would require them to create, or at least modify, the law that would settle the case. Therefore, when such an unsettled case comes before a court of law, the decision judges reach cannot be described as one that *applies* the law, because there is no relevant law to apply. In such unsettled cases, the court's ruling amounts to a modification of the law; it is an act of creating new law, akin to other familiar ways in which law is created or modified by legislatures and other legal authorities. This idea, that law is bound to run out—and therefore that judges would need to participate in the creation of new law by way of judicial legislation—has been labeled the doctrine of *judicial discretion.*

In a famous article criticizing Hart's theory of law, Ronald Dworkin has argued that the doctrine of judicial discretion is fundamentally flawed.[1] The gist of Dworkin's argument is simple: Hart wrongly assumed, Dworkin claimed, that the law consists only of rules. But in addition to legal rules, which are typically enacted by legal authorities (as Hart assumed), there is another type of legal norms, which Dworkin called *legal principles*, which do not derive their legal validity from any particular enactment. Legal principles gain their legal validity by a process of reasoning, including moral reasoning, and not by decree.

In order to understand Dworkin's argument, it is essential to realize that there are two main conclusions he wanted to draw from the idea that there are legal principles: first, that the law does not run out, and therefore judges do not have the kind of discretion Hart envisaged; and second, that there is a distinct class of legal norms that cannot derive its legal validity from Hart's rules of recognition. Underlying both of these conclusions is the idea that the legal validity of principles partly, but necessarily, depends on some truths about morality; it is partly a matter of moral truths that some norms are legally valid and form part of the law. Let me briefly explain these points.

Dworkin begins the argument by suggesting that the distinction between legal rules and legal principles is a categorical one: Rules operate in a kind of "all or nothing" fashion; if a rule applies to the circumstances, it determines a legal outcome. If an outcome is not determined by a rule, then it must be because the rule does not really apply to the case at hand. Contrary to this, principles do not necessarily determine an outcome; if a principle applies

---

[1] Dworkin, "The Model of Rules I," in *Taking Rights Seriously*, chap. 1.

to the circumstances, it only provides a reason to decide the case one way or the other. Principles have a dimension of weight: The reasons they constitute may weigh more or less under the relevant circumstances, depending on various considerations.[2] To illustrate, consider, for example, a rule that determines the maximum speed limit on a given highway and the accompanying traffic offense if one exceeds the limit. If I drive on that highway, the rule clearly applies to me, and therefore the outcome is determined: If I exceed the speed limit, I have committed the offense. Now compare such a rule with the legal principle judges sometimes employ in their decisions (to take one of Dworkin's favorite examples): that a person should not be allowed to profit from his own wrong. As every lawyer knows, however, such a general principle does not quite determine legal outcomes. The law sometimes allows people to profit from a wrong they have committed.[3] The role of such principles is subtler: to provide judges and other legal agents with reasons to make certain decisions in doubtful or borderline cases. If there is a choice to be made, as it were, and one of the options would allow a person to profit from his own wrong, then the principle counts against allowing such an outcome. But, by itself, the principle does not dictate the outcome—certainly not in every case in which a person may profit from his wrongs.

Some philosophers have doubted, however, that the distinction Dworkin had in mind is really a categorical one, that is, between two different types of legal norms. It may be much more natural to think of it in terms of a distinction in degree, one that is on a continuum between, at one end, legal norms that are very specific and, at the other end, norms that are very general and/or particularly vague.[4] Naturally, the more general a legal rule is, the more exceptions and modifications to it one should expect. Thus, according to this line of thought the relevant difference between the rule that determines the speed limit on the highway and the rule that stipulates that people should not be allowed to profit from

[2] Dworkin noted several other differences (ibid.), but they are all entailed by the underlying distinction between rules that determine a legal outcome and principles that only provide reasons for an outcome.

[3] Gaining property rights by adverse possession is a good example.

[4] In the legal literature, this distinction is between "rules" and "standards."

their own wrongs, is one of degree of generality: The former applies to a very specific set of circumstances; the latter applies to a very wide range of possible circumstances. Given the latter's generality, it should come as no surprise that the law would have to recognize many exceptions and modifications to the general rule.

I think this criticism of Dworkin's distinction is in the right direction, but the truth is that, by itself, it does not quite undermine his main argument. The main argument depends on Dworkin's additional thesis pertaining to the ways in which rules and principles gain their legal validity. Legal rules, Dworkin claims, typically gain their validity by an act of enactment, more or less along the lines presumed by Hart and other legal positivists. Legal principles, however, are not enacted. They are deduced by reasoning from certain facts and, crucially, moral considerations. How is that? Suppose, for example, that a court is faced with a problematic case that would seem to be unsettled by the existing legal rules; as far as we can tell, no previously recognized law would settle the case. In such cases judges can, as they often do, reason in the following way: They would look at the legal history of the settled law in the relevant legal area (such as previous precedents, statutes, and regulations) and then try to figure out what are the best moral principles that would justify the bulk of those settled cases. The general principle that forms *the best moral justification* of the relevant body of law *is* the legal principle that would bear on the case at hand. In other words, we conclude that a legal principle forms part of the law by a process of reasoning. We start by observing the relevant legal facts that are established by previous law and then try to reason to the principle that forms the best moral justification of this body of law. The conclusion of this reasoning—which is partly, but essentially, a moral one—is a legal principle, one that forms part of the law.

So now we can see why Dworkin concludes both that the law never quite runs out and that legal principles are such that they cannot derive their legal validity from anything like the rules of recognition. The law never quite runs out simply because the kind of reasoning that leads to legal principles is one that is always available. Whenever judges might think that existing law does not settle the case they face, the judges can reason their way to the solution by the same process; they can always ask themselves what would be the best moral justification of the relevant body of law and apply the principle that forms the answer to this question to the case at hand.[5] At the very least, it should give the court a reason, a legal reason, to decide the case one way or another. So there is always some law that applies, namely, the general principle that constitutes the best moral justification of previous decisions in the relevant area.

The idea that legal principles are partly deduced by reasoning also shows why these norms cannot gain their legal validity by reference to the rules of recognition in the way Hart had envisaged. Principles do not become part of the law because an authority has decided that they do; their legal validity is partly, but necessarily, a matter of moral truths. A given principle, say P, is part of the law if and only if P actually constitutes the best moral justification of previous legal decisions. P's legal validity, therefore, depends on some truths about what constitutes the best moral justification of previous decisions. Legal validity is thus partly a matter of moral truth.

Dworkin's thesis about legal principles has attracted an enormous amount of attention over the years. Many objections and modifications have been offered, but it has been generally conceded that Dworkin succeeded in showing something of great importance, both about the ways in which judges, especially in the common law tradition, reason to resolve hard cases, and about the diversity of norms that form part of our legal landscape. Legal philosophers who were more sympathetic to Hart's legal positivism, however, resisted both of the conclusions that Dworkin wanted to draw from the existence of legal principles. Some have argued that law may run out even if there are legal principles, while others argued that legal principles, though perhaps distinct from legal rules, are nevertheless such that their validity can be accounted for on the basis of Hart's rules of recognition.[6]

---

[5] To complete the argument, one would have to assume that morality does not run out. But that would not be a question-begging assumption.

[6] See, e.g., Raz, "Legal Principles and the Limits of Law"; and Coleman, *The Practice of Principle*, 103–7.

I have some doubts about both of these reactions to Dworkin's argument. If Dworkin is right about the fact that norms can gain their legal validity by the type of reasoning he suggests, then the conclusions he draws would seem to be perfectly sound.[7] The main question, therefore, is whether there are legal principles or not. To be more precise, the question is whether what Dworkin describes is really a way in which judges *identify what the law is*; or is it better to describe it as a form of judicial reasoning leading judges to *create new law* or at least to modify the existing law, in order to settle new cases?

Think about it this way: Suppose it is true that whenever judges face a case that would seem to be unsettled by the existing body of law, they reason to the solution in the way Dworkin describes, namely, they look at the relevant body of previous decisions and try to figure out the best moral justification of those decisions. And once they come up with such a justifying principle, they apply it to resolve the case at hand. So far, none of this would show that the principle the judges have settled on is one that had been part of the law prior to their decision. This story is equally compatible with the view that the identified principle becomes part of the law because, and only because, of the judicial decision that applies it. In other words, the story is compatible with the view that Dworkin simply described one main way in which judges modify the law or create new law; the relevant principle becomes part of the law only due to the authority judges have to modify the law by their judicial decisions (if, and to the extent, of course, that they have such an authority). Prior to the judicial decision that identifies a certain principle as a legal one, the principle had not actually formed part of the law. It only becomes law when judges say that it is, and only because they say so. And this interpretation would be perfectly in line with the general idea that the law consists of authoritative directives.

---

[7] To be historically more accurate, it is fair to say that some of the confusion was due to the fact that, in his original article on legal principles, "The Model of Rules I," Dworkin was not entirely clear about the ways in which legal principles become part of the law. His argument was clarified years later, particularly in *Law's Empire*.

In order to rebut this objection, Dworkin would have had to show that the judicial reasoning that leads to the identification of a certain principle as a legal one is reasoning about what the law had been prior to the decision—that it is a form of reasoning purporting to discover, as it were, what the law is, and not, as I suggest, reasoning about ways in which the law needs to be changed. As far as I can tell, however, the only argument Dworkin presents to support his interpretation is an appeal to judicial rhetoric.[8] When judges apply a legal principle to bear on the cases they adjudicate, they tend *to say* that they just apply a principle that had always been the law, not that they invent a new principle that they favor (morally or otherwise). But this appeal to rhetoric is problematic, at best. First, it is a double-edged sword: Judges sometimes state very clearly that they see their role as one of creating new law, not applying existing law, since they think that there is no law to apply. If you take judicial rhetoric seriously, you cannot pick and choose the rhetoric that favors your interpretation; the rhetoric goes both ways. More importantly, however, the problem is that even when judges say that they simply apply the law as they find it—no matter how circuitous the road that leads there might have been—one would often have very good reasons to doubt that judges actually believe what they say. This is a political problem. The institutional role of judges in making law is a politically contentious issue. People normally expect the legislatures to make the law and the judges to apply it. Recognizing the fact that judges often have to make the law that they apply to the case at hand is not something that sits easily with the popular conception of division of power between legislatures and the courts. I am not claiming that it is a secret that judges often make new law—far from it. But it has the status of an inconvenient truth, so to speak, widely recognized as it is. And this inconvenience puts judges under considerable pressure to coat the making of new law in the rhetoric of law application. Caveat emptor is the legal principle that should be applied to judicial rhetoric.

Still, you may wonder, is there any consideration that supports the alternative interpretation, whereby principles become part of

[8] See Dworkin, *Law's Empire*, chap. 1.

the law only because judges make it the case, by their authoritative decisions, that they are legal norms? Consider this possibility: Suppose a court—and let us take the U.S. Supreme Court as our example here—faces a difficult case that would seem to be unsettled by existing law. And suppose the justices on the court reason exactly in the way Dworkin suggests they do. However, let us assume that different justices on the court come up with different results. Suppose that five justices conclude that the relevant principle that would bear on the case is M, and four justices conclude that the principle is actually N. And let us assume that M and N are mutually exclusive under the circumstances, namely, that if principle M applies, then it entails that not-N, and vice versa. As it happens, principle M gains majority support and therefore the ruling is according to M. Let us further assume that the majority has made a *moral* mistake; principle N is the one that, all things considered, morally speaking, should have been applied. What is the law now? Every lawyer would tell you that, at least until the ruling is overturned by a subsequent decision, the law is M. It may not be a good law, certainly not the best, but it is the law. And it is the law because in the U.S. legal system, the Supreme Court has the authority to determine what the law is in such cases, and it is also the law that the court's legally binding decision is the one that is supported by the majority of its members.

Such examples cannot prove that Dworkin's thesis is mistaken. According to his thesis, the conclusion would have to be that the majority has made a legal error in this case. That, of course, is possible; any reasonable theory about the nature of law should allow for the possibility that a court would render a ruling that is legally mistaken. Let us suppose, however, that the case I described here is not a singular occurrence, but the general pattern. In other words, it is certainly possible to envisage a legal system, not unlike the ones we are familiar with, in which the Supreme Court systematically errs on the moral considerations it relies upon and ends up endorsing principles that are not, morally speaking, the best or the most appropriate—they do not form the morally best interpretation of the relevant body of law. If you endorse Dworkin's thesis, you will end up with the conclusion that a great deal of the law—or, at least, of what people take to be the law—in a given legal system is legally mistaken. Surely, at some point one would have to doubt whether a theory that renders a great part of the law to be a legal error is really a theory that tells us what the law is.

I am not trying to replicate the age-old argument that even a morally wicked legal system is still law. The examples I have in mind need not go that far; they do not have to assume that the legal system in question is morally iniquitous—far from it. The argument works even if we assume that the courts tend to get the moral considerations underlying the legal principles they adopt just slightly off, so to speak. According to Dworkin's thesis, they would have still made a legal error; and then again, the result we get is that a substantial part of the law is legally mistaken. At the very least, such a result should count against the kind of theory that entails it.

Inclusive Legal Positivism

The general idea that the content of the law cannot be detached from moral truths has gained considerable support even within the legal positivist tradition. Many contemporary legal positivists tend to deny the thesis that law only consists of authoritative decisions. It is quite possible, they argue, that moral considerations would also bear on what counts as valid legal content, or legally valid norms, in a given legal system. It is not necessary that this be the case, they argue, but it is certainly possible. This new version of legal positivism has been labeled *inclusive legal positivism*, and it has several variants. The underlying thesis is that it is possible for a given legal system to have norms that incorporate various moral considerations judges and other officials would have to rely on in determining what the law is. And, in such cases, the argument is, the law partly is what the true moral considerations entail. Thus, it is at least possible for some truths about morality to determine what the law is.

Different versions of inclusive legal positivism have different views about the kinds of norms that could incorporate morality into law. I think that there are two main versions of this view.

One maintains that law can incorporate moral conditions on legal validity explicitly—simply by decreeing so. Some familiar provisions of written constitutional documents might provide good examples. The U.S. Constitution, for instance, contains references to such moral concepts as equality, cruelty, and due process. The German Basic Law contains an important provision that all laws must respect human dignity. Etcetera. Etcetera. So it seems that there are cases in which the law, typically in a constitutional document, explicitly makes the legal validity of other parts of the law conditional on some moral truths.

The second, and I think more prevalent, version of inclusive legal positivism maintains that morality can be incorporated into law in a more profound way, that is, by the content of *the rules of recognition* that happens to prevail in a given legal system. It is possible to have a legal system in which the rules of recognition that are practiced by the relevant legal community are such that they make the legal validity of some subset of the law depend on certain moral requirements or moral conditions, or such.[9]

It seems that the first version, though much more simple and straightforward, does not gain much support among philosophers, and for good reasons. An explicit statutory or constitutional reference to moral considerations does not make it the case that it is really moral truths that determine what counts as law. It only means that judges and other legal officials have to take moral considerations into account when they make an authoritative decision about what the law is. Joseph Raz explained how this works by introducing the notion of *directed power*. Legal officials have powers to determine various legal outcomes and, more often than not, this power is directed by considerations they need to take into account in the exercise of their legal powers. An authority may have the legal power, for example, to grant building permits; typically, this is a very circumscribed power, and it is legally directed. The relevant official is instructed to rely on certain types of considerations, while excluding other types, in granting or refusing to grant the permits. She may consider, for instance,

---

[9] This is the version of inclusive positivism suggested by Coleman, "Negative and Positive Positivism," and Waluchow, *Inclusive Legal Positivism*.

environmental considerations, but not, say, religious ones. And, of course, there is nothing to prevent the law from directing the power of its officials, judges included, by reference to certain moral considerations.

None of this would show, however, that morality becomes part of the law. Consider, for example, a case in which an official—say, the city architect—is granted the legal power to refuse certain building permits on aesthetic grounds—say, if the proposed building would be "aesthetically incongruous" with the buildings in its vicinity. Surely, we would not want to say that in this case aesthetics becomes part of the law, or that truths about what is "pretty" form part of what counts as law. It is true that the official's decision can be legally challenged, inter alia, on aesthetic grounds. A dissatisfied party might file an appeal, for instance, challenging the architect's official decision on grounds that it was aesthetically mistaken, and such an appeal might win the day. There is nothing unique about this. Official decisions can be challenged legally on numerous grounds, such as economics, justice, morality, bureaucratic efficiency, or whatever, but only if the challenge succeeds, that is, if a higher legal authority decides that it succeeds, then it is law.

The suggestion that the rules of recognition can incorporate morality as a condition of legal validity is much more interesting and at least initially plausible. The idea is this: We can envisage a certain community in which the rules of recognition establish certain recognized ways of making law but only on the condition that the enacted law is not grossly immoral, or that it does not violate basic human rights, or such. Now, if such a rule of recognition is possible, then it would seem that moral constraints form an essential part of the conditions of legal validity. Law would be valid only if it meets certain moral constraints. And this would be the case because, and only because, this is the rule of recognition that happens to be practiced in the relevant population. Inclusive legal positivists argue that there is nothing that precludes such a possibility. It is, they say, at least conceptually possible. And if it is conceptually possible, then it is possible for truths about morality or justice to form part of what the law is.

There is a very clear sense in which the inclusive version of legal positivism aims to have the cake and eat it at the same time.

It purports to remain faithful to the basic tenet of legal positivism that what the law in any given society is, is basically determined by social rules; yet it also purports to incorporate some of Dworkin's insights about the nature of legal reasoning, whereby the content of law is sometimes determined by moral truths. Whether this combination is possible turned out to generate a huge debate in contemporary legal philosophy,[10] but one that may have given contemporary analytical jurisprudence a bad name. It is difficult to avoid the impression that the debate degenerated to hair-splitting arguments about something that makes very little difference to begin with. Since I participated in this debate, I am not sure that I can share this view. But it might be best to avoid a summary here of the hair-splitting arguments that have emerged for and against inclusive legal positivism, and focus on some of the main questions instead.

First, it may be worth noting that inclusive legal positivism must discard the idea that the rules of recognition are social conventions. A conventionalist account of these rules does not sit easily with the idea that they can incorporate morality as part of what the rules prescribe. To illustrate the problem, consider a very different setting: We have certain conventions about appropriate modes of conduct at various social events, such as, for example, a dinner party. So there is a convention that you need to bring something, such as flowers or a bottle of wine, to the dinner party you attend. Or that you need to eat with silverware (and not, say, with your hands), or such. But it would be very odd to suggest that there is a convention that you have to behave well, morally speaking, during the dinner party. Reasons to behave morally well are there independently of any conventions. Conventions do not establish moral reasons for action. Conventions are norms that evolve to resolve cases in which the relevant social norms are underdetermined by reasons. If reasons completely determine the content of their corresponding norms, the norm is not a convention. And the same idea applies to the rules of recognition. If such rules are social conventions, it is odd to suggest that they also incorporate moral norms. But this is not a conclusive argument

---

[10] See, e.g., Coleman, *The Practice of Principle*, part 2; Himma, "Inclusive Legal Positivism," 105; and my contribution on "Exclusive Legal Positivism," 104.

against inclusive positivism, since the latter can simply deny that the rules of recognition are conventional in nature.

Another issue, more widely recognized in the literature, is the problem of reconciling the inclusive version of positivism with the view—shared by many of its adherents—that law is, by and large, an authoritative institution. Joseph Raz famously argued that it would make no sense to maintain that a directive is authoritative if the subjects of the authority would have to rely on moral considerations in order to determine what the content of the authoritative directive is. The whole point of having an authoritative resolution is that the subjects are presumed to better act on the reasons that apply to them by following the authority's directive than by trying to figure out (or act on) those reasons by themselves. If the subjects have to employ the same kinds of reasons that the authority was meant to rely on when issuing its directive in order to figure out what the directive is, then the whole point of having an authority would seem to be missed. From this argument, Raz concluded that both inclusive legal positivism and Dworkin's legal theory cannot be true, because they both fail to realize that it makes no sense to have a practical authority if one can only identify what the authority decrees by relying on the same kinds of reasons that the authority was meant to replace.[11]

Inclusive legal positivism has two kinds of possible answers to Raz's argument: One line of thought challenges the general idea that each and every legal norm must be understood as an authoritative directive. The other rejoinder concedes that legal norms have to be understood as authoritative, but argues that Raz is wrong to assume that the authoritative nature of law is somehow undermined by the idea that sometimes we may need a moral argument to determine what the law is. Both types of rejoinders have been defended in the literature, sometimes with great ingenuity (or perhaps even a bit too much of it). I will not try to summarize these complicated arguments here, partly because I think that the main difficulty with inclusive legal positivism is the same difficulty we encountered with respect to Dworkin's thesis about legal principles. Both views, and for the same reason, entail the

[11] Raz, "Authority, Law, and Morality."

possibility that a substantial part of the law in a given legal system amounts to a legal error. And this makes very little sense. In fact, it makes even less sense on the basis of the inclusive version of legal positivism than on Dworkin's account. Dworkin, after all, denies that legality ultimately depends on some social rules. In fact, as we shall see in the next section, Dworkin came to deny that an intelligible distinction exists between what the law is and what morality would require the law to be. So at least in the context of Dworkin's theory, the idea that a whole legal community might be mistaken about the true content of its laws would make some theoretical sense. But if you subscribe to the positivist tenet that legality is, ultimately, a matter of social rules, then the idea that an entire community might get its laws wrong becomes mysterious, at best.

LAW AS INTERPRETATION

We have so far tried to examine whether the content of the law may sometimes depend on certain considerations about what that content ought to be, as a matter of moral truth. Whatever the answer, we assumed that there is, at least in principle, a general distinction between what the law *is* and what it *ought* to be; or that it would make perfect sense to say that the law on issue X is P, but from a moral perspective, it ought to have been Q, and Q entails not-P. In his more recent writings on the nature of law, Dworkin began to challenge the soundness of this basic distinction. In fact, his elaborate arguments, based on the interpretative nature of law, aim to show why the distinction between what the law is and what it ought to be is much less clear than we have assumed all along. What the law is, Dworkin claims, is *always* a matter of evaluative considerations, moral ones included. Dworkin's argument is very complex, partly because it is not only an argument about the nature of law, but is also an argument about the nature of legal theory. As we shall see in the next chapter, Dworkin quite clearly rejects the possibility of any descriptive jurisprudence, that is, of any general philosophical theory that purports to describe the nature of law. Jurisprudence, in Dworkin's view, is partly, but essentially, normative political philosophy. A moral-political justification of the legitimacy of law is a necessary part of any attempt to explain what law is.

Underlying both of these major challenges to traditional analytical jurisprudence is the concept of interpretation. Law is thoroughly interpretative in its nature, and any attempt to explicate this interpretative enterprise is also an interpretation. Although these two levels of interpretation are, according to Dworkin, inextricably linked, I think that we must proceed in stages. In this chapter I will briefly explain how Dworkin concludes that the content of the law is always a matter of evaluative/moral judgments. The methodological challenges will be taken up in the next chapter.

Although Dworkin's arguments are very complex, the basic idea is enchantingly simple. And it can be summed up in the following framework argument:

(1) Every conclusion about what the law requires, in any given case, is necessarily a result of interpretation.

(2) Interpretation is, essentially, an attempt to present its object as the best possible example of the kind or genre it belongs to.

(3) Therefore, interpretation necessarily involves evaluative considerations, and of two main kinds: considerations about the values inherent in the relevant genre, and evaluative considerations about the elements of the object of interpretation that best exhibit those values.

(4) From (1) and (3) it follows that every conclusion about what the law is necessarily involves evaluative considerations. What we deem the law to be always depends on our views about the values we associate with the relevant legal domain and ways in which those values are best exemplified in the norms under consideration.

Clearly if (4) is correct, then the traditional distinction between questions about what the content of the law actually is and what that content ought to be cannot be separated. The only way to understand what the content of the law is, is by reference to the kinds of content it ought to have under the circumstances. And if this general idea is true, then legal positivism, in all its forms, is patently false.

There are two crucial premises in this framework argument: first, that every conclusion about the content of the law is a result of interpretation; and, second, that the very nature of an interpretation is such that it necessarily involves evaluative considerations. If both of these premises are true, then conclusion (4) would certainly follow. Let me state from the outset that I think there is a great deal of truth in the second premise, but the first premise is false, and thus the argument as a whole, fails. But we need to see how the arguments play out. So let us start with some of Dworkin's views about the nature of interpretation in general and then see how they apply to the nature of law.

What is interpretation? A fairly safe starting point is to assume that we interpret a certain utterance or a text, and so forth, when we try to figure out its meaning. Interpretation is typically an attempt to understand what something means. At least in some contexts, such as in an ordinary conversation, the relevant meaning we are interested in consists in what *the speaker* (or the author of the text) meant by saying or expressing this or that. And certainly this might be the case in the legal context as well. On the Pacific Coast Highway running through Malibu, there are a few signposts with the following inscription: DRUNK DRIVER CALL 911. When you stop laughing, you realize that the people who put up the signpost must have meant that, if you observe a driver who might be drunk, you should call 911 and inform the police. It is very unlikely, you tell yourself, that the authorities expected drunken drivers to call 911. It is just not what they meant.

However, it is widely assumed that in many contexts, particularly in the realm of the arts, and perhaps in the context of interpretation of social practices, interpretation is not necessarily an attempt to understand what the author/speaker actually meant by the relevant expression or text. Even if we know what the author meant, some interpretative questions may remain open. Or we might not be particularly interested in the author's intention; or there might not even be an author. But then the difficult question to answer is what is it that we are interested in instead? If interpretation does not strive to grasp what the author meant, what other meaning might be in play? Dworkin proposed a very interesting answer to this question, which he called constructive interpretation:

> Interpretation of works of art and social practices, I shall argue, is indeed essentially concerned with purpose not cause. But the purposes in play are not (fundamentally) those of some author but of the interpreter. Roughly, *constructive interpretation is a matter of imposing purpose on an object or practice in order to make of it the best possible example of the form or genre to which it is taken to belong.*

And, as Dworkin immediately clarifies: "It does not follow . . . that an interpreter can make of a practice or a work of art anything he would have wanted it to be . . . the history or shape of a practice or object constrains the available interpretation of it."[12]

There are three main insights about the nature of interpretation that are present here: first, that interpretation strives to present its object in its best possible light, as the best possible example of the genre to which it is taken to belong; second, that interpretation is essentially genre dependent and in ways that explain why interpretation is necessarily an evaluative form of reasoning; and finally, that there are certain constraints that determine the limits of possible interpretations of a given object. I will not have much to say here on this last point, since it raises many complicated issues that would take us too far from our concerns. My main aim is to explain the first two theses. So let us begin with the obvious question: Why *the best*? Why should interpretation of an object or text strive to present it in its *best possible* light? One who expects a detailed, argumentative answer to this crucial question is bound to be disappointed. Dworkin only offers two clues to his answer. The first clue is in a footnote: An interpreter is bound to strive for the best possible presentation of the object of interpretation, Dworkin claims, because "otherwise we are left with no sense of why he claims the reading he does."[13] The other line of thought is less direct, deriving from Dworkin's assumption that

---

[12] Dworkin, *Law's Empire,* 52 (my emphasis).

[13] Ibid., 421n12.

the only alternative to this constructive model is the traditional author's-intention model, which he rejects for various reasons. So let us take up these two points in turn.

Perhaps Dworkin's intuition is clear enough: If two interpretations of, say, a novel, can be put forward and, according to one of them, the novel emerges in a better light—that is, as a better novel—it would seem to be rather pointless if we insisted on rejecting that interpretation in favor of the one that presents the novel in a worse light. This is the kind of intuition we are familiar with from a philosophical argument as well. If you want to criticize someone's thesis, you are not going to convince anyone of the cogency of your critique unless you have tried to present the object of your critique in its best possible light. It does not mean, of course, that anything you try to interpret must be presented as something valuable or particularly successful. But unless you try to make the best of it first, there is little hope in convincing anyone that it is a failure.

The only possible alternative Dworkin sees to this heuristic assumption is the author's-intention model. According to this model, interpretation is nothing but an attempt to retrieve the actual intention, purpose, and such, that the author of the relevant text had with respect to various aspects of its meaning. Therefore, if the assumption is that what the text means is only what its author intended it to mean, then, of course, the question of presenting the text in its best light does not arise. For better or worse, the interpretation of the text would only consist in whatever it is that we can find out about the author's intention. If a better reading of the text is available, that would be an interesting critique, perhaps, but not an interpretation of it. So it seems that in order to substantiate the central thesis of the constructive model of interpretation, Dworkin must refute its obvious rival, the author's-intention model. Or, at least, this is what Dworkin's assumes.

Dworkin has two main arguments against the author's-intention model of interpretation. The first argument—which draws most of its intuitive support from examples in the realm of works of art—relies on the fact that artists typically intend their works to become cultural entities, detached from their original intentions and purposes. Once a work of art had been created, the artist would rather have it stand on its own and speak for it-self, as it were. Thus, at least in the realm of the arts, it will often happen that the attempt to apply the author's-intention model of interpretation would turn out to be self-defeating. You think that the text means what the author intended it to mean, so you seek out the author's intention only to find out that she had intended her intention to be ignored. Perhaps it is not accurate to say that this just may happen. Perhaps it is something deeper about the nature of art or, at least, art in the modern world, that works of art are typically created with such an intention to become cultural entities, detached, at least to some extent, from the artists' par-ticular intentions. But there are two serious problems with this argument. First, even in the realm of works of art, there is nothing necessary or essential to Dworkin's characterization. Some art-ists may simply not share the kind of vision it involves. So this self-defeating argument might defeat itself. If you argue that the author's intention should be ignored because it is the intention of the author that it should, you may find out that the intention you rely upon does not exist; perhaps the author of your text actually wanted his particular intention to be relevant for the interpreta-tion of his work. Why would you ignore that intention now?

More importantly, the argument is based on the ways in which artists tend to view their creative activities and on certain aspects of the nature of art. But then it is questionable that the argument can be extended to other cases. In particular, it is doubtful that the argument can be extended to the realm of law without beg-ging the question against its factual assumptions. Is it safe to as-sume that those who create legal texts, such as legislators and judges, also tend to share this intention that their intentions not be taken into account? It is very doubtful that they do.[14] Thus, if there is a general argument against the author's-intention model, it must be a different kind of argument. Trying to refute the

[14] There is an ongoing debate in U.S. constitutional law, for example, about the potential relevance of the framers' intentions about the constitutional provisions they drafted. Many American jurists share Dworkin's view that the answer to this question depends on the intentions of the framers about their intentions. There-fore, a great deal of historical research is brought to bear on this debate, and it remains inconclusive, at best.

author's-intention model on the basis of assumptions about authors' intentions is just too precarious and unstable.

Dworkin does have another argument against the author's-intention model that is more nuanced and insightful. In order to understand it, however, we need to get a better sense of the ways in which interpretation is genre dependent. An interpretation, according to Dworkin, strives to present its object as the best possible example of its kind, that is, of the genre to which it is taken to belong. This assumes that it is impossible to interpret anything without first having a sense of what kind of thing it is—what is the genre to which it belongs. On the face of it, this may sound too rigid; after all, sometimes we do seem to be engaged in an interpretation of a text or object even if we are not quite sure what the appropriate generic affiliation of the text is. And sometimes the appropriate generic affiliation is precisely what is at dispute between rival interpretations of an object. An interpreter may argue, for instance, that Samuel Beckett's *Mercier and Camier* is best read as a play, and another may think that it is actually a novel. Dworkin, however, need not deny any of this. Even when the generic affiliation is the issue, one would still have to decide which affiliation presents the work as a better work of literature, for example. In other words, when the specific generic affiliation is not clear, we need to ascend in a level of abstraction and try to decide which generic affiliation of the text would present it as a better example of the higher-level affiliation, say, as a piece of literature or, if that is in doubt, as a work of art, and so forth. In any case, we must have a sense of what kind of thing it is that we strive to interpret, even if the classification is tentative or rather abstract.

There is a deeper insight here. We can only interpret a text if we have a sense of what kind of text it is, because we must also have a view about the values that are inherent in that kind or genre. Unless we know what makes texts in that genre better or worse, we cannot even begin to interpret the text. You cannot begin to think about the interpretation of a novel without having some views about what it is that makes novels good (or bad), and you cannot interpret a poem without having a sense of the values we find in poetry (or, in poetry of that kind), and so on. If you propose a certain interpretation of a novel, for example, you must rely on some views you have about the kinds of values that make novels good and worthy of our appreciation. Otherwise you could not explain why we should pay attention to the kind of interpretation you propose—why pay attention to the aspects of the work you point out and not to any other? So I think that Dworkin is quite right to maintain that, without having some views about the values inherent in the genre to which the text is taken to belong, no interpretation can get off the ground. The values we associate with the genre partly, but crucially, determine what would make sense to say about the text—what are the kinds of meaning we could ascribe to it.

This insight also explains, however, the real nature of the debate about author's intention in interpretation. As Dworkin explains,

> the academic argument about author's intention should be seen as a particularly abstract and theoretical argument about where value lies in art. . . . I am not arguing that the author's intention theory of artistic interpretation is wrong (or right), but that whether it is wrong or right and what it means . . . must turn on the plausibility of some more fundamental assumption about why works of art have the value their presentation presupposes.[15]

This is very important. Those who maintain that the particular intention of, say, a novelist, has a bearing on what the novel means, must also maintain certain views about what makes novels valuable and worthy of our appreciation. They must think that understanding what the author strove to achieve, or the message the author wanted to convey, are the kinds of considerations that bear on the novel's meaning, which also assumes that they are the kinds of considerations that are related to what makes novels valuable, and vice versa, of course. If you deny the relevance of the novelist's intention, that is only because you have certain views about what makes novels valuable—views that are detached from the values we associate with the communication aspects of literature, or perhaps art in general. Needless to say, art is just

[15] Dworkin, *Law's Empire*, 60–61.

an example here. A very similar line of reasoning applies to the possible roles of the intentions of legislatures in the interpretation of statutes and the possible role of the framers' intentions in the context of constitutional interpretation. Whether it makes sense to defer to such intentions must also depend on a theoretical argument about where value lies in the relevant genre, namely, the authority of legislation or the authority and legitimacy of a constitution.[16]

Thus the conclusion so far is that the author's-intention model of interpretation only makes sense as an instance or an application of the constructive model. It does not compete with it. Whether it makes sense to defer to the intention of the author or not is a local issue, specific to the genre in question, and depending on the values we associate with the latter. Does it prove Dworkin's point that interpretation must always strive to present its object as *the best* possible example of the genre to which it is taken to belong? It would prove the point only if we agreed with Dworkin that the only alternative to the traditional author's-intention model is the constructive model. But this is a questionable assumption. Interpretations need not strive to present the text in its best possible light; they could simply strive to present it in a certain light, perhaps better than some, worse than others, but in a way that highlights an aspect of the meaning of the text that may be worth paying attention to for some reason or other. Let us recall that Dworkin's insistence on "the best" derives from the assumption that, unless one strives to present the text in its best light, "we are left with no sense of why he claims the reading he does."[17] But this simply need not be the case. And sometimes it just cannot be the case. Let me clarify. There are two points here: one about the motivation and interest in various interpretations, and the other about the limited possibilities of an all-things-considered judgment about what is the best.

First let us address motivations. Dworkin's assumption that, unless one strives to present the text in its best light, we would

---

[16] I have explained this in much greater detail in my *Interpretation and Legal Theory*, chaps. 8 and 9.

[17] See note 13, above.

have no reason to pay attention to the interpretation offered, is just not true. We are familiar with many interpretations, in the realm of works of art, and others, where we have a very good sense of why the interpretation is interesting and worth paying attention to, even if it does not purport to present the text in its best light. For example, a psychoanalytical interpretation of *Hamlet* would be very interesting and certainly worth paying attention to, even if it does not necessarily render the play better than other, more traditional interpretations of it. It simply brings out a certain aspect of the play that is interesting on its own right. Perhaps it contributes to a better understanding of Shakespeare's work, highlighting aspects of it hitherto unnoticed, enriching our understanding of the subtleties and richness of the work, and so forth. It can do all this without assuming that the particular interpretation offered presents *Hamlet* in its best possible light. And the same thing can be said about, say, a modern adaptation of *Hamlet* set in a contemporary setting, or perhaps even a parody of it. Thus the general assumption that, without striving to present the text in its best light, we would have no sense of why the interpretation is worth paying attention to, is simply groundless.

Regardless of the question of motivation, however, there is also a question about possibilities. As several commentators have pointed out,[18] Dworkin's insistence on the best possible light rests on the assumption that in each and every case there is the possibility of an all-things-considered judgment about what makes a given work valuable—what makes it the best possible example of the genre to which it is taken to belong. But this assumption, it is rightly claimed, ignores the problem of incommensurability. It is a rather prevalent aspect of the evaluative dimensions of works of art, and many other possible objects of interpretation, that often there is no possibility of rendering an all-things-considered judgment about their relative merits. There is simply no such thing as *the best*. Some interpretations may be better, or worse, than others, but none could be claimed to be the best. That is so, at least in part, because some of the evaluative comparisons are incommensurable. The incommensurability of values

[18] See, e.g., Finnis, "On Reason and Authority in *Law's Empire*."

consists in the fact that there are certain evaluative comparisons in which it is not true that A is better than B, and not true that A is worse than B, and not true that A is equal to or on par with B. That is typically so because A and B are mixed goods, composed of numerous evaluative dimensions, and they just do not have a sufficiently robust common denominator that makes an all-things-considered judgment possible. Numerous things make novels valuable, for instance, and one interpretation may render the novel more valuable on a certain dimension, while another interpretation may make it more valuable on other dimensions. Often it would be simply impossible to say which one of them, all things considered, is better (or worse), and not because there is something we do not know, but because the relevant comparisons are essentially incommensurable.

If this is so obvious, why does Dworkin deny it (as he does)? What is it in Dworkin's theory that makes him insist on the possibility of presenting an object of interpretation in its *best* possible light, that is, all things considered? I think that the answer to this puzzle is to be found in Dworkin's jurisprudence, not in his general theory of interpretation. The latter makes perfect sense without this problematic element. As we saw in the previous section, Dworkin's earlier thesis about legal principles assumes the same basic idea: A principle forms part of the law, he argued, if it constitutes the best possible justification of the relevant body of law. If there is no "best, all things considered," the whole idea becomes extremely problematic because we might end up with the conclusion that different, even contradictory, principles would be best under certain assumptions, which would entail the conclusion that, even on Dworkin's account, law is profoundly indeterminate. Thus, unless Dworkin assumes that there is the best, all things considered, we would have come a long way only to see that Hart was right after all, and judicial discretion is inevitable.

Be this as it may, I think that Dworkin is right about one important issue: He is certainly correct to point out that interpretation is, essentially, a kind of reasoning or understanding that depends on various evaluative considerations. You cannot propose an interpretation of a text or an object without making certain assumptions about what makes texts of that kind better or worse; 107

a certain evaluative conception about the kinds of interests we have in the text under consideration and the kinds of values we associate with texts of that kind, is part of what makes interpretations possible. But this does not yet prove Dworkin's main point about the nature of law and its necessary relation to morality. The latter depends on the first premise of his framework argument—that every conclusion about what the law is, or what it requires, is a result of some interpretation or other. In other words, it is a crucial assumption of Dworkin's interpretative theory of law that it is never the case that a legal instruction can simply be understood, and applied, without any interpretative process involved. And this is a problematic assumption, to say the least. It calls into question a great deal of what philosophy of language teaches us about meaning and language use, in general. As I will try to show in chapter 6, Dworkin's assumptions about the nature of language and the ubiquity of interpretation are not sustainable. But before we get to this, we need to consider the methodological challenges to Hart's theory of law, and this is the topic of the next chapter.

Suggested Further Readings

Cohen, *Ronald Dworkin and Contemporary Jurisprudence.*
Coleman, *The Practice of Principle.*
Dworkin, *Law's Empire.*
Marmor, *Interpretation and Legal Theory.*
Marmor, ed., *Law and Interpretation: Essays in Legal Philosophy.*
Raz, *Ethics in the Public Domain.*

Is Legal Philosophy Normative?

H.L.A. HART famously characterized his theory about the nature of law as "descriptive and morally neutral."[1] Hart, like previous legal positivists such as John Austin and Hans Kelsen,[2] thought that a philosophical account of the nature of law should strive to avoid moralizing of any kind, and should aim at an explanation of the nature of law that is quite general in its application—one that explains what law, in general, is. Clearly there are at least two assumptions here. First, it is assumed that, in spite of variations between different legal systems across time and place, law is a fairly universal phenomenon in human societies, and that it has certain features that are essential or characteristic of law, as such. Second, it is assumed that we can identify and articulate those essential features of law without forming any moral or political judgment about the merits of law or any particular legal institution. Understanding what law is, is one thing; judging its merits is quite another.

Many contemporary legal philosophers have come to doubt this theoretical aspiration. They claim that a theory about the nature of law, such as Hart's legal positivism, cannot be detached from moral and political views about law's merits. We cannot understand what law is, they claim, without relying on some views about what makes law good and worthy of our appreciation. The clearest example of such a methodological view is Ronald Dworkin's recent interpretative theory of law. Dworkin

---

[1] This chapter is based on my article "Legal Positivism: Still Descriptive and Morally Neutral," 683, and appears here in a revised form.

[2] Although not Bentham. As Gerald Postema demonstrated convincingly, Bentham did not share this view. See his *Bentham and the Common Law Tradition*.

quite explicitly presents his own theory of law as a moral-political theory. As he made clear in *Law's Empire*, his assumption is that the main moral-political question about law is the question about the legitimacy of coercion: What is it that would justify the use of collective force to enforce political decisions of certain kinds? The justification for the use of collective force is the main moral question that underlies, according to Dworkin, theories about the nature of law. In one way or another they aim to provide an account of law, an interpretation of our practices, which would answer this moral-political question. Other critics of Hart are not necessarily committed to Dworkin's view about the main moral question at issue, but they share Dworkin's general methodological point. Even Hart's legal positivism, they claim, is, ultimately, a normative theory because it can only be defended on normative, moral-political grounds. This methodological challenge to legal positivism forms the topic of this chapter. I will argue that Hart was quite right, and that it is both possible and theoretically desirable to detach a philosophical account of the nature of law from moral and political views about law's merit.

Normative Legal Positivism

The idea that legal positivism is not detachable from its underlying moral concerns came to be called "normative legal positivism." There are, however, at least five possible views about the relations between normative claims and legal positivism. Not all of them are necessarily opposed to the thesis I wish to defend. In order to give a basic account of these five views, let me assume that there is some core descriptive content of legal positivism, and let me stipulate that P stands for this core descriptive content, whatever it is. Accordingly, here are the five positions I have in mind:

(1) *It ought to be that* P (*or something roughly coextensive with* P).

To the extent that ought implies can, such a view would also be committed to the thesis that P is a real possibility—that it can actually be materialized, at least to some significant extent. But the main focus of this version of normative positivism is on the moral-political domain. It argues that legal positivism is a good thing, that it ought to be materialized in a free and democratic society, for instance, because it is a practice of law that best promotes the goods favored by such a theory. I take it that this is basically the view propounded by Tom Campbell[3] and, following Campbell, I will call it *ethical positivism*.

(2) *It is the case that* P, *and it is morally-politically good if it is generally recognized that* P.

I believe that this is the position held by H.L.A. Hart. He thought that legal positivism, as a general theory about the nature of law, is basically descriptive and morally neutral. However, Hart also believed that a general, public recognition of the truth of *P* would free us from romanticizing myths, and thus enable a more critical attitude toward law that is not just theoretically correct but also morally-politically beneficial.[4]

(3) *It is the case that* P, *and it is a good thing, too.*

Perhaps at some point Hart may have held such a view as well. He seems to have indicated that not just a general recognition of *P* is morally good, but also certain aspects of the content of *P* are morally good (though this is not quite accurate, as we shall see below).

(4) *The law ought to be a morally legitimate institution; for law to meet conditions of moral legitimacy, it should be the case that* F; F *entails* P, *therefore it is the case that* P.

Dworkin's account of what he calls "legal conventionalism" is a prominent example of such a view. In *Law's Empire*, Dworkin understands legal conventionalism to be a partly normative theory with descriptive conclusions—a theory that purports to reach conclusions about the nature of law on the basis of some

---

[3] See Campbell, *The Legal Theory of Ethical Positivism*.

[4] See Hart, *The Concept of Law*, 205–6. If I understand MacCormick correctly, this is one of the main arguments he also makes in "A Moralistic Case for A-Moralistic Law?" However, at points MacCormick seems also to endorse a version of the argument of type 3.

normative moral-political ideals. I will call this view *substantive normative positivism*.[5]

(5) *Determining whether it is the case that* P *or not-*P *necessarily relies on some normative, moral-political claims.*

This is a methodological view about the nature of jurisprudence. As such, it purports to refute Hart's claim that general jurisprudence *can* be purely descriptive and morally neutral. According to this view, then, part of the debate between positivism and its opponents necessarily boils down to a normative one and, if legal positivism can be defended, it must rest, inter alia, on some normative—moral-political—claims.

My aim is to show that the first two versions of normative positivism do not threaten Hart's claim that legal positivism is a descriptive and morally neutral theory about the nature of law. The third view is crucially ambiguous—in one sense it may be problematic; in another, and the one that Hart actually maintained, it is not. Mostly, however, I will focus on the latter two versions of normative positivism—the substantive and the methodological—arguing that they are wrong, both as expositions of legal positivism and as critiques of it.

Before we proceed, it is important to clarify what descriptive legal positivism does *not* amount to—what is not in dispute or, at least, should not be. First, as many contemporary legal positivists have repeatedly emphasized, legal positivism has no theoretical reasons to deny that the law is a good thing, that we have good reasons to have law and have flourishing legal systems.[6] Whether the law, as such, has any intrinsic value may well be controversial. But positivism certainly concedes that the law has considerable instrumental value and, therefore, whenever the reasons to use law are present, law would be instrumentally valuable or instrumentally good. Furthermore, legal positivism can concede that the law is necessarily good, if it is true that human nature, or the nature of human society, is such that makes it necessary to have

[5] One may wonder how this view differs from ethical legal positivism. I will try to explain this in the section titled "Substantive Normative Legal Positivism."
[6] See, e.g., Gardner, "Legal Positivism: 5 1/2 Myths."

law. If E is an end we necessarily have, and L is a necessary instrument to achieve E, then L is necessarily good, even though L is still valuable only instrumentally. I am not claiming that this is the case, only that legal positivism has no theoretical reason to oppose it.

Second, legal positivism has no reason to deny that law's *content* necessarily overlaps with morality. It may well be the case that every legal system, immoral or wicked as it may be, would necessarily have some morally acceptable content, or that it would necessarily promote some moral goods.[7]

Finally, consider this quotation (from Campbell): "In legal theory, Legal Positivism is generally taken to be the view that the concept of law can be elucidated without reference to morality, and that it is the duty of judges to determine the content of and apply the law without recourse to moral judgments."[8] Both parts of this claim are potentially misleading, and it is important to see why. First, I doubt that legal positivists have ever held the view that the concept of law can be elucidated "without reference to morality." Legal positivism is a view about the nature of law. It purports to understand and explain what the law is, what makes it a special instrument of social control, how it figures in our practical reasoning, and what makes it the kind of social institution that it is. None of this can be understood without a great deal of knowledge about the numerous functions and purposes the law serves in our culture. Generally speaking, you cannot even begin to understand a social practice without knowing what it is there for—what it is that it is supposed to do. Without an understanding of the essential functions, or rationale, of a social practice or institution, it would be hopeless to attempt a theoretical understanding of it. It is not difficult to see that law has moral and political functions in our society. It is there to solve, among

---

[7] Why necessarily? The idea would have to be that a form of regime or de facto authority that is completely wicked and promotes absolutely nothing of value could not be recognized as a legal order—would simply not function as law, so to speak. I am not sure about this argument, and I certainly do not wish to defend it here. I tend to think that this is contingently true as a rough generalization, but not necessarily.

[8] Campbell, *Legal Theory of Ethical Positivism*, 69.

other things, moral and political problems. Therefore, it would be futile, if not meaningless, to try to elucidate the nature of law in terms that do not employ moral concepts and do not involve an understanding of the kinds of moral and political problems the law is there to solve.

The question of whether such reliance on understanding of moral issues necessarily implicates a philosophy of law with normative-evaluative claims is a separate one, and I will consider it in some detail below. But it would be a mistake to begin with the assumption that legal positivism purports to be an account of the concept of law (that I take to stand for an account of the nature of law) that could be reduced to a language that contains no moral terms and has no reference to morality. That just cannot be done, and I am very doubtful that any legal positivist thought otherwise.[9] Once again, to clarify, I do want to deny that an understanding of the moral and political concepts essential for an understanding of the nature of law necessarily implicates jurisprudence with any particular moral-political stance or moral-political evaluations. But this is certainly not tantamount to the idea that legal positivism purports to account for the nature of law "without reference to morality."[10] I will say much more about this crucial distinction later on.

The second part of the quotation from Campbell is also rather misleading. Legal positivism is not a theory about the moral duty of judges. Whether judges have a moral duty to apply the law in any given case is a moral question that can only be answered on moral grounds. Furthermore, no legal positivist of whom I am aware has ever suggested that judges need to set aside morality in their official judicial roles. A judicial role is not a vacation from moral responsibilities. Perhaps this is the source of the confusion: As noted in the previous chapter, Hart, and other legal positivists, have repeatedly emphasized that the law often runs out, and then judges have no other option but to rely on their best (sometimes moral) judgment in order to determine the case at hand, or

---

[9] With the exception, perhaps, of John Austin.

[10] Unless by "reference to morality" one means a reliance on moral judgments and evaluations.

in order to determine how to change the law and modify it. But from this it in no way follows that, when the law *is* clear, judges have a *moral* duty to apply it. They may trivially have a legal duty,[11] but the question of whether there is a moral duty to follow a legal obligation is always open, even for judges, and should normally be determined on moral grounds.

ETHICAL POSITIVISM AND THE ETHICS OF POSITIVISM

Let us assume, for now, that the core content of a legal positivist theory about the nature of law is more or less along the lines described in the previous chapters, or, at least, that we have some agreement about what that core content is. The methodological question therefore is whether this core content can be viewed from a normative perspective or, indeed, whether it is, somehow, partly normative by necessity. I will have very little to say here about Campbell's ethical positivism or any such similar view. Quite explicitly, Campbell does not purport to argue for the truth of legal positivism as a theory about the nature of law. He argues for a moral-political stance that would require a certain vision of law and legal practice that accords with what he takes legal positivism to be. In short, ethical positivism is a political theory, not a theory about the nature of law.

The only relevant point about ethical positivism that we have to notice is that it is not at odds with the view I want to defend here—that legal positivism, as a theory about the nature of law, is basically descriptive and morally neutral. Ethical positivism does not deny this claim because it does not compete with it. "It ought to be that *P*" is perfectly consistent with the proposition that "It is the case that *P*" or that "It is a fact that *P*." True, the more obvious it is that *P*, the less interesting it may become to insist that it ought to be that *P*. But again, this is not something for us to worry about here. Generally speaking, the truth of a

---

[11] Not necessarily, though. Even when the law is clear, it may be the case that judges are not under a legal duty to apply it to the particular case at hand; they may still have the legal power to change the law.

descriptive proposition is not affected by the interest in its moral, normative endorsement.

H.L.A. Hart's normative endorsement of legal positivism's descriptive content is quite different. Hart occasionally mentioned the following type of normative claim: It is the case that P, and we are better off recognizing it as such.[12] Hart clearly thought that P consists in a description of social facts, and a sobering one at that. Hart believed that the more we can come to realize that legal validity and morality are not necessarily or conceptually linked, the easier it is to subject the law to critical appraisal. It is crucial to note, however, that Hart has never thought that the descriptive content of his claims about the nature of law somehow derives from the fact that it is morally or politically beneficial to believe in those facts and recognize their importance. And rightly so, since it is all too clearly a non sequitur. From the fact that "It is morally good that everybody believes that P," it does not follow that P.[13]

Perhaps there is a more general suspicion that looms large here: Looking at the various legal theories on offer, one would quickly observe that almost every theory about the nature of law is accompanied by its normative endorsement by its author. They all seem to claim that it is the case that Q and, in some sense, this is a good thing, too. One might then suspect that the theory's claim that Q is actually motivated by the presumed moral-political appeal of Q, or the moral advantage of recognizing Q's truth. It would be difficult and, in any case, pointless, to deny that descriptive theories, particularly about such a normative domain as law, are often motivated by the normative assumptions of their authors. But there are two points to remember here. First, in a sense this is more generally so, that is, not only with respect to

---

[12] See, e.g., Hart's *The Concept of Law*, at 205–6, and his *Essays in Jurisprudence and Philosophy*, 72–78.

[13] Note that we assume that P is a set of descriptive propositions. At points, one may get the impression that MacCormick, in "A Moralistic Case for A-Moralistic Law?," actually makes this mistake of inferring that P from the thesis that it is morally good if everybody believes that P. But it is not always clear that he takes P to consist of descriptive propositions. In other words, one can interpret MacCormick as advancing a form of ethical positivism.

normative preconceptions. It is often the case that we first have a sense of a philosophical conclusion before we can articulate the arguments that support it. Rational deliberation is always an ongoing negotiation between conclusions that seem right to us and the arguments or evidence that would support them. The essence of dogmatism is the refusal to revise one's initial, unreflective conclusions in light of contrary evidence. One essential purpose of criticism and philosophical scrutiny is to resist dogmatism. And that is the best we can hope for. We cannot eschew our theoretical or moral preconceptions, but we should always try to subject them to scrutiny, and we should always be willing to revise our initial conclusions in light of contrary evidence.

Second, and more to the point, it is, again, undeniable that legal theories emerge from a particular intellectual and political background, and are often motivated, more or less explicitly, by a moral-political vision. For example, as Gerald Postema has convincingly demonstrated, Bentham's legal positivism formed part of his moral-political agenda and was considerably motivated by Bentham's utilitarianism and his aspiration for legal reform.[14] Similarly, it is probably the case that Hart's concerns about the relations between law and morality, and the debates about his views at the time, were partly shaped by the intellectual concerns of the post–World War II era. Crudely put, the manifest legalism of the Nazi regime, and the practical need to judge its perpetrators ex post facto, evoked a serious dilemma: either to admit that law can be profoundly evil or to deny that such morally heinous law can be law at all. For those who sought a legalistic justification of the Nuremburg trials, the latter option seemed to offer a neat solution: The Nazi perpetrators could not seek to shelter themselves under the law that they had allegedly complied with at the time, if such wicked law is not law at all.[15]

---

[14] See Postema, *Bentham and the Common Law Tradition*. Furthermore, Postema argues it is not entirely clear that Bentham was sufficiently aware of the distinction between an account of law *as it is* and his arguments about how to make law more useful or beneficial (331).

[15] These kinds of concerns resurfaced with the collapse of the Berlin Wall and the decision to prosecute former East German guards who had "shot to kill" escapees to the West, allegedly following the legal orders of the regime at the time.

Hart clearly thought that this solution was wrong, and that we would better learn the lessons of the Nazi regime by coming to realize that law is not necessarily just—that the law can be morally heinous and still be law. Hart thought that this was an important and sobering political lesson we should learn from jurisprudence, and that we would be on safer grounds, morally and politically, to be alert to the fact that legality is never a guarantee of justice or moral soundness. That such views partly motivated Hart's legal positivism I have no doubt. And that I happen to share these views I have no qualms to admit. But this neither shows that legal positivism is, in any interesting sense, a normative theory, nor does it show that the truth of its descriptive content depends on the truth of its normative motivation, to the extent that there is one.

Put in simple terms: A descriptive theory about the nature of law makes a claim to truth. The only philosophically relevant question about a philosophical description is whether its claim to truth is warranted or not—whether it is, actually, true. The intellectual and historical background of such a theory, whether moral, political, or other, may help us to a better sense of the content of the theory, but it does not bear on its truth. The motivation for claiming that P is one thing, and the truth of P is another. The former is the business of intellectual historians. Philosophy should be interested in truth.

Another normative aspect in Hart's theory may seem more problematic, and this is the third version of normative positivism I have mentioned. At points it seems that Hart claimed not only that a general recognition of P's truth is morally good, but that certain aspects of the content of P are good as well. Of particular concern is chapter 5 of *The Concept of Law*. As we saw in chapter 3, one of Hart's most important claims about the nature of law is that any developed legal system is a union of primary and secondary rules. In chapter 5 of *The Concept of Law*, where he presents this thesis, Hart seems to be making the additional claim that this is a good thing, too, because the addition of secondary rules remedies certain defects of a rudimentary legal system that would only be composed of primary rules. Thus, the addition

of secondary rules makes the law more developed and better in serving its social functions. Jeremy Waldron and Stephen Perry understand this argument as a normative one. It "gives the lie to Hart's claim to be engaged in purely descriptive jurisprudence," Waldron says.[16]

It is easy to misunderstand Hart's claim because it is ambiguous. Consider the difference between the following two propositions:

(1) L is x, and this makes L good.
(2) L is x, and this makes it good L.

If Hart had made a claim of type (1), perhaps we should have been worried about his mixing a description of law with its normative appraisal.[17] But Hart clearly makes a claim of type (2). His claim is not that the development of secondary rules makes the law a better institution—morally more legitimate, so to speak. Hart simply claims that the development of secondary rules enables the law to better serve its functions; it makes it more efficient, qua law. This is perfectly consistent with the claim that the law just is whatever it is, regardless of its moral merit, or that it is not necessarily good to have more, rather than less, efficiency in law's functioning. In other words, this is not a normative claim in the relevant sense. That a knife is sharp, for example, does not make the knife good in any normative-moral sense of "good." It just makes it a good knife; better suited for its putative function.[18]

Some philosophers claim that any view about law's essential functions, or purposes, renders it normative; and since, as we have already admitted, no plausible theory about the nature of law can avoid such claims about law's functions in society, they

---

[16] See Waldron, "Normative (or Ethical) Positivism," 429. See also Perry, "Hart's Methodological Positivism," 323ff.

[17] Even in this case, however, much would depend on the exact content of the claim. As I have earlier indicated, legal positivism is compatible with the thesis that law is necessarily good.

[18] Hart himself made it quite clear that such functional values are not necessarily moral or normative in the relevant sense, in his reply to Fuller's thesis about the rule of law virtues. See his *Essays in Jurisprudence and Philosophy*, 349–50. By this I do not mean to endorse Hart's view that the virtues of the rule of law are purely functional. In fact, I have criticized this view in my "The Rule of Law and Its Limits," in my *Law in the Age of Pluralism*, chap. 1.

conclude that any theory about the nature of law must rest on some normative assumptions, legal positivism included. I will examine this claim in some detail below.

SUBSTANTIVE NORMATIVE LEGAL POSITIVISM

In chapter 4 of *Law's Empire*, Dworkin purports to present an interpretation of legal positivism that he calls "conventionalism" on normative grounds. One immediate problem with it, however, is that very few legal positivists would recognize their work in this chapter. Since Dworkin does not attribute conventionalism to any particular theorist (none is mentioned in this chapter), perhaps he just invented this view as a friendly suggestion. If so, I believe that we need to say thanks, but no thanks. Here is why.

"The heart of any positive conception of law," Dworkin claims, "is its answer to the question why past politics is decisive of present rights."[19] Assuming that this is the main question, conventionalism is presented as a possible answer: "Past political decisions justify coercion because, and therefore only when, they give fair warning by making the occasions of coercion depend on plain facts available to all rather than on fresh judgments of political morality, which different judges might make differently."[20]

This line of thought relies on Dworkin's thesis that the central question in jurisprudence is how to justify the use of collective force by the state, and how to justify the fact that certain forms of past political decisions warrant such use of coercive force, and to what extent.[21] Legal positivism is then presented as a possible answer to this question. So here is the argument, as I see it:

(1) The law ought to be a legitimate institution.
(2) In order to account for law's legitimacy, we must provide an answer to the question of why past political decisions justify the use of collective force.

---

[19] Dworkin, *Law's Empire*, 117.
[20] Ibid.
[21] Ibid., 114.

(3) Legal positivism claims that the answer to the question in (2) is given by the ideal of protected expectations.

(4) The relevant kinds of expectations can be adequately protected only if law entirely depends on conventional sources.

(5) Therefore, tying the identification of law to conventional sources is the best interpretation of legal practice.

There are two ways to read this argument. One is to see it as a form of what we have called ethical legal positivism—as a moral-political argument of the form, *it ought to be that* P. It would then be an argument that recommends something like legal positivism from the perspective of a political theory—a prescriptive account about the role of law in society, and about how law should be practiced in order to be morally legitimate. As I have already argued, however, ethical positivism does not compete with descriptive jurisprudence and, therefore, cannot refute it either. And I do not think that this is what Dworkin had in mind. Conventionalism is presented by Dworkin as a possible, albeit eventually wrong, *interpretation* of legal practice, not simply as a recommendation about the way law ought to be practiced.

But then there is a serious problem: How can we get to a descriptive conclusion from answering a question about moral legitimacy? In other words, even if we follow Dworkin's argument until step (4), the move to step (5) remains a bit of a mystery. If (5) purports to have a descriptive content, this could not follow from (4). *It ought to be that* P simply does not entail that *P*. (Note that if (5) is understood in prescriptive terms, we are back to ethical positivism and its irrelevance to our concerns.) Of course, it would have been a different argument if we replace premise (1) with—

(1a) The law is a legitimate institution.

Then perhaps something like (5) could somehow follow—not straightforwardly, but perhaps as a possible interpretation of law's legitimacy. But this is a kind of assumption that legal positivism cannot endorse. No theory that begins with the assumption that law is a morally legitimate, or justified, institution can possibly be associated with legal positivism of any kind. One of the most important insights of legal positivism is that law is a social-political instrument and that, as such, it can be used for good or bad purposes—it can be used legitimately or illegitimately. Of course, we can have a theory about what would render the law in this or that context legitimate, but this would not be a theory about the nature of law. It would be part of a moral-political theory about what constitutes good or justified law, not about what law is.

To sum up the problem: If we begin with a question about what would make law legitimate, we cannot end up with conclusions about what the law is. And if we begin with the assumption that the law is legitimate, we are no longer in the realm of legal positivism (or any other descriptive legal theory, for that matter).

Undoubtedly, Dworkin would reply that I have ignored his account of what interpretation is, and how interpretation of such a practice as law necessarily combines elements of description and evaluation. I will get to this in a moment, when we consider Dworkin's version of the methodological argument, in the next section.

THE METHODOLOGICAL ARGUMENTS

In his postscript to *The Concept of Law*, Hart reemphasized that his account of the nature of law is "descriptive in that it is morally neutral and has no justificatory aims; it does not seek to justify or commend on moral or other grounds the forms and structures which appear in my account of law."[22] The upshot of the methodological arguments I want to consider is that this aspiration is conceptually misguided and, in any case, not attainable. Any jurisprudential account of the nature of law must be premised on moral and other evaluative views about the law. There are three main versions of this argument. The first, propounded by Stephen Perry, rests on the necessity to account for the functions of law. The second argument, espoused by Dworkin, Michael Moore, and Waldron, focuses on the nature of the enterprise and its

[22] Hart, *The Concept of Law*, 2nd ed., 240.

essentially evaluative presuppositions. And the last, suggested by all four scholars and others, focuses on Hart's own idea about the internal point of view and its importance for understanding law. I will consider these three arguments in this order and I will try to show that they all fail, and for similar reasons.

The Argument from Function

Perry's argument is best captured by this quotation:

> Jurisprudence requires a conceptual framework. The difficulty is that the data can plausibly be conceptualized in more than one way, and choosing among conceptualizations seems to require the attribution to law of a point or function. This in turn involves not just evaluative considerations, but moral argument.[23]

I have already conceded the first main premise of this argument. It is, indeed, the case that we cannot possibly understand such a complex social practice as law without an elaborate understanding of its essential functions in society. The only question that remains is why would it be necessary to engage in moral argument in order to understand the main functions of law, or its point, as Perry suggests?

Let us suppose that we want to understand a social practice, largely as Hart suggests, constituted by social rules or conventions. Perry is quite right to assume that knowing the rules would not suffice to explain the practice. At the very least, we must also understand their point. For example, we cannot hope to understand the game of chess without understanding, more generally, what games are and what the point is of playing them. We must understand, among other things, that the participants aim to win the game, which means that we must understand the complex idea of winning (or losing) a game and such subtleties as winning it decisively, or gracefully, or barely winning, and so forth. In other words, it is certainly true that an understanding of a normative social practice, such as law, games, and such, must comprise

---

[23] Perry, "Interpretation and Methodology in Legal Theory," 123.

an understanding of its functions, or points, and often of the values that would render intelligible the participants' relevant beliefs in their reasons for action. Needless to say, these purposes and beliefs can be put to critical scrutiny. One may wish to say that the putative values are not worth pursuing, that they are foolish or wrong, or that the practice may have had other, better values worth pursuing instead. But this kind of criticism is just an option that a critic may decide to pursue, or not. It is one thing to understand what the game of chess is and quite another to decide whether it is a good idea to play it or not.

Consider, for example, a straightforward functional explanation of a social rule. Suppose we can show that the function, or rationale, of a social rule, say R, in a given society S, is to solve a recurrent coordination problem that members of S face under circumstances C. Solving the recurrent coordination problem is what explains the rationale of following rule R in society S under circumstances C. Such an explanation would typically rely on certain propositions about matters of fact, such as the nature of the relevant circumstances, people's actual beliefs and preferences, and the function, or the rationale, of the rule in their practical reason, given those factual assumptions. I find it very difficult to see, however, where the moral argument is hidden here. The explanation need not contend that the coordination problem that rule R is there to solve is one that *ought* to be solved, morally speaking, or that it *morally justifies* following R. It only explains the function of R for members of S, given their circumstances, preferences, and the like. A descriptive account of the functions of a social practice need not rely on any particular views about the moral merit or worth of the functions or purposes that would make sense of the practice in question.

Perry's argument rests on the assumption that an account of the functions of a practice like law is either a "causal explanation of some kind" or "moral in character: it is grounded in a certain understanding of the moral point or value of the institution of law."[24] But this is clearly a false dichotomy, and actually in two respects. First, the "point or value" of an institution need

[24] Ibid., 114.

not be moral. Countless activities and practices serve a point or value, but those values have nothing to do with morality. Arguably, some of the points or values of legal institutions may have little, if anything, to do with moral concerns. Second, and more importantly, even if we suggest that an institution serves some moral values, it does not follow that an account of those values and how they rationalize the institution in question is, in itself, a moral account. Suppose, for example, that I ask myself what is the point or purpose of our greeting conventions; and suppose that I suggest that their point has something to do with the need to manifest respect or show some recognition of the worth of our acquaintances. I have not offered anything that can be called a moral justification of the practice of greeting conventions. I may well hold the view that showing respect in this way is not morally warranted—that it is not a purpose morally worth pursuing. In other words, a functional explanation of the moral point or purpose of a certain practice would not fail if it were the case that, morally speaking, the practice is not warranted. Such an explanation would only fail if it happens to be false, as a matter of fact.

Perhaps the false dichotomy Perry relies upon derives from a certain ambiguity in the way we use functional explanations. Consider, for example, ways in which we employ the idea of usefulness. Sometimes when we say that "X is useful," we intend to express a positive endorsement of X's purpose. For example, if somebody says, "cell phones are very useful," it would be natural to assume that the speaker believes or implies that cell phones serve some good purposes. But this is not always and not necessarily the case. By suggesting, for example, that the sharpness of the knife makes it more useful, we are not committed to an evaluation of its uses. A sharp knife is more useful in cutting bread, and is also more useful in killing a person. In short, functional explanations do not necessarily commit the explanation to an endorsement of the object's putative functions.[25]

---

[25] Although she does not focus on Perry's arguments, Julie Dickson has advanced a very similar line of reasoning against this methodological challenge in her *Evaluation and Legal Theory*.

The Argument from Interpretation

This false dichotomy between causal explanations and moral evaluation of a social practice sometimes informs Dworkin's methodological argument as well.[26] But I believe that we can present a clearer version of it without this fallacy. Jeremy Waldron suggests such a version, and it relies on three main premises. First, that it is a central issue in jurisprudence to determine whether certain types of normative claims are legal or not—whether they form part of the law or not. Second, that such disputes cannot be rendered sensible without "testing the respective theories against our sense of why it is important whether something counts as law or not."[27] Third, Waldron maintains that an answer to this "Why" question is bound to be normative; it is bound to rely on certain views about what makes law good and worthy of our appreciation. Therefore, Waldron concludes, jurisprudence necessarily relies on normative considerations.[28]

This is a very important argument, and it is almost persuasive. In fact, I think that the first two premises are quite right. Undeniably, it is a central question in jurisprudence, what makes certain types of normative claims legal and others not. This is, basically, what the dispute over the conditions of legal validity boils down to. We want to understand what makes certain norms legally valid. And I think that Waldron is right to insist that such a theoretical dispute can only make sense on the background of some understandings about why it is important—why would it matter whether something is a legal norm, or not? So let me propose

---

[26] Dworkin, *Law's Empire*, 64.

[27] Waldron, "Normative (or Ethical) Positivism," 420.

[28] Ibid. At one point Waldron is unnecessarily too hard on himself. He thinks that this argument commits him to the view that "in order to do positivist jurisprudence in the normative mode, one has to view law *as a good thing*" (428), and he rightly wonders whether this is not too strong. But I do not see how he is committed to this strong view at all. All that the argument commits him to (as opposed to Dworkin's argument, perhaps), is to say that normative positivism must have some views about what would make law good or bad—views that would explain why it is important to distinguish legal from other normative claims. This is not tantamount to viewing law as a good thing. Suppose that somebody thinks that law is actually a bad thing. That would give him a very good reason to strive to distinguish what law is from what it is not.

an answer: It matters to us, as theoretical observers, because we want to *understand what the law is*, as distinguished from other types of norms, and from what the law ought to be. (Note that for participants in the practice, for the subjects of a legal order, it may matter for other reasons; I will get to this shortly.)

Now you may think that I am just pushing the question one step further. Why would we want to understand what the law is in this respect, as opposed to countless other questions we could have asked instead? Is this not a normative stance? Well, not more than any other quest for theoretical understanding. Theoretical questions always arise in the background of certain assumptions about what it is that needs explanation. Our sense of what needs explanation is typically path dependent, emerging from the history of the discipline and certain views that have been collectively shaped over time about what is theoretically or practically important.[29] Admittedly, any views about relative importance are partly normative, but if this is the only sense of normativity that Waldron has in mind, surely that would be too trivial. Any theory, in any given realm, is normative in *this* respect. There is, however, nothing in Waldron's argument to support the conclusion that we cannot come to understand the theoretical importance of articulating a theory about legal validity without a moral explanation of the quest for understanding. Why should our interest in the nature of law be necessarily guided by moral concerns?

Dworkin may have an interesting answer to this. It combines an emphasis on the interpretative nature of jurisprudence with the evaluative, normative nature of the practice it purports to interpret. Let me explain. The upshot of Dworkin's methodological argument is very simple. First, it assumes that jurisprudence is necessarily an interpretation of law (as a social practice). Second, it argues that all interpretations, as such, are essentially value laden. As we saw in the previous chapter, interpretation, by its very nature, necessarily relies on evaluative judgments. Therefore, jurisprudence is necessarily evaluative.

One way to object to this reasoning is to reject its first premise, because it seems to trade on a crucial ambiguity. There is a broad sense of "interpretation" that would certainly make it plausible

---

[29] See, e.g., Raz, *Engaging Reason*, 159.

to claim that any philosophical account of the nature of law is necessarily interpretative. But in this broad, relaxed sense of "interpretation," just about any theoretical explanation would be interpretative. Think of a zoologist who tries to figure out why apes spend so much time grooming one another. Surely, in a clear sense, the zoologist is trying to interpret the apes' behavior. Alternatively, "interpretation" can be understood much more narrowly, along the lines suggested by Dworkin's *constructive model.* Now the problem is that, in the former case, the point has not been proved, since it is not clear that any interpretation in this broad sense is necessarily evaluative. (Think of our zoologist, again. She is not evaluating anything; she just tries to figure out the biological functions of the apes' behavior. She is certainly not trying to present their behavior in its best light.) Yet if we assume a narrow, partly evaluative meaning of "interpretation," it is far from clear that we must concede that any philosophical account of the nature of law is necessarily "interpretative." I think that this is a serious worry, but I will not push it any further here. Dworkin's argument fails, even if we generously grant (most of) its main premises.

As noted in the previous chapter, one of Dworkin's most important insights about interpretation consists in the way he regards evaluations essential to any interpretative project. One cannot even begin to interpret a text, he rightly claims, without first forming a view about the values that are inherent in the genre to which the relevant text belongs. After all, how can I begin to form an interpretation of, say, a novel, without having a pretty good idea about what makes novels good or bad, better than others, and the like? A certain vision of what the values inherent in the genre are is essential to any attempt to interpret texts that belong to that genre. The interpreter, Dworkin claims, must form an evaluative judgment of her own about those values that are inherent in the practice she purports to interpret. Such judgments, Dworkin claims, are not essentially different from the evaluative judgments of the practitioners themselves.[30]

---

[30] Dworkin, *Law's Empire*, 64. A very similar point is made by Waldron in "Normative (or Ethical) Positivism," 425–26.

This last move, however, is not so smooth, at least with respect to social practices such as law. There is a crucial difference between forming a view about values that are inherent in a certain practice—that is, values that would rationalize the practice for its participants—and having an evaluative judgment about them. An anthropologist may form the theoretical view that a certain rite is valuable for the people who practice it because it enhances their social cohesion—without having any particular judgment about the value of social cohesion, certainly not one that is somehow competitive with her subjects' evaluative judgments. Similarly, a legal philosopher may suggest that the law is an essentially authoritative institution, without a commitment to any particular views about the legitimacy of legal authorities or their moral worth. Forming a theoretical view about a purpose or value that explains a given practice is not the same as forming an evaluative judgment about it—nor is the latter entailed by the former.

Arguably, different kinds of theoretical explanations of social practices face different methodological constraints. Presumably, it would not necessarily count against a causal-scientific explanation of some form of human behavior that the relevant subjects could not possibly come to recognize the explanation as something that rationalizes their conduct. It is possible that a philosophical explanation is different in this respect. Perhaps a philosophical analysis must be such that it explains the practice in terms that the participants could, at least in principle, recognize as something that explains to them what the point of their practice is. Even so, the explanation need not be one that is based on moral or other normative judgments that compete with the judgments of the participants, to the extent that they have any.

In other words, there is a crucial difference between grasping a value and having an evaluative judgment about it. People can comprehend the values held by others, understand the point of those values—their relevance, and such—without forming any judgment of their own about those values. I can understand, for instance, that the glorification of Catholicism formed an essential purpose of the Counter-Reformation baroque architecture, without admiring Catholicism (or baroque for that matter) myself, or actually having any particular evaluative judgment about these evaluative schemes.

Well, in one obvious sense this is not quite accurate. Our understanding of values is limited by our own past experience and conceptual-evaluative scheme. Sometimes people can come to understand new values by learning, but this is a relatively rare occurrence, it takes time and effort, and learning may not succeed. Does this mean that there are values of alien cultures that we could never come to understand? Not necessarily.[31] It does mean, however, that learning new values is relative to what we already know and to the values with which we are already familiar, and this certainly renders our ability to grasp values somewhat limited and dependent on our own experience and culture. Nevertheless, the distinction between grasping a value and having an evaluative judgment about it still holds. The fact that our ability to understand values or practices of other cultures is limited by our own cultural-evaluative background does not entail that understanding necessarily collapses into judgment (of the relevant kind). And, if this distinction holds, it becomes very difficult to understand why jurisprudence, as an attempt to understand a social practice, must be engaged in moral evaluations of the kind Dworkin and Waldron envisage.

The Argument from the Internal Point of View

It is possible to take the argument from interpretation one step further. Many legal philosophers maintain that it makes a crucial difference that the practice we aim to understand is itself a normative practice—one that purports to guide peoples' conduct and form reasons for their action. After all, it was Hart who introduced to legal philosophy the idea that an adequate explanation of law must take into account the "internal point of view," that is, the normative point of view of the participants in the practice. Committed participants, mostly judges and other officials, regard the rules of law as reasons for action. Therefore, they must regard the law as valuable or justified, at least in some respect.

[31] See, e.g., Raz, *Engaging Reason*, 157.

This is undeniably true. It is true that we cannot attain an adequate understanding of the law without taking into account the perspectives of committed participants, and it is also true that committed, active participants typically regard the law as something that gives them reasons for action. No doubt, the internal point of view is normative, at least partly in a moral political sense.[32] But it still remains to be shown why a philosophical understanding of such a normative point of view would be committed to taking any stance on the values or normative assumptions it purports to explain. Why can it not remain essentially descriptive and morally neutral? As you may recall from chapter 3, Hart's main point about the internal point of view was actually to show that recognizing the importance of the internal point of view does not preclude a reductive explanation of it. We can explain how the law guides the conduct of its subjects by explaining how the subjects regard legal instructions as reasons for their actions. And we can do that without endorsing their evaluative perspective.

Consider the analogy with the deliberation of a particular individual. Suppose that we want to understand why Sarah engages in a certain activity—say, of regularly attending concerts at the Los Angeles Philharmonic. It would be very difficult to make sense of her conduct without having a sense of her individual perspective: she may have reasons to be interested in classical music, or perhaps she just values the social interaction at the concert hall, and that may form a sufficient reason for her to attend. Either way, an account of her actions would have to be based on her reasons for action. But do I need to judge those reasons from my own evaluative perspective? Would my account of Sarah's reasoning

---

[32] Hart, actually, resisted this last conclusion, at least as it is understood in moral terms. Hart insisted that even "when judges . . . make committed statements . . . it is not the case that they must necessarily believe that they are referring to a species of moral obligation." See his *Essays on Bentham*, 161. I have some doubts about the point of this debate. If we assume, as seems plausible, that a reason for φ-ing entails that φ is valuable, or that φ-ing will bring about something valuable, then committed participants must be taken to presume that the reasons for following the law are reasons that derive from some values the law promotes. I tend to think that it matters very little whether we classify these values as necessarily "moral" or not. Morality has very fuzzy boundaries anyway.

necessarily rely on evaluative judgments at all, or some evaluative judgments competitive with hers? Nothing seems to compel such a conclusion. Once again, the opposite view seems to follow from a confusion between grasping a value or an evaluative reasoning and forming an evaluative judgment about it. As I have already conceded, there are some inherent limits to values and evaluative reasoning we can grasp. To some extent, our ability to understand such things is shaped and limited by our own evaluative schemes and cultural habituation. But this is not the same, not even close, to the conclusion that any understanding of evaluative reasoning collapses into judgment.

Dworkin's reply is not difficult to surmise. My attempt to explain Sarah's reasoning is an interpretation, he would say, and, as such, it must purport to present its object in its *best possible light*, as the best possible example of the kind it belongs to. An attempt to present something in its best possible light, all things considered, necessarily relies on evaluative judgments of the kind that would be competitive with the judgments or reasoning one purports to interpret. But here we must part company. As I have argued in the previous chapter, the assumption that interpretation, by its very nature, must present its object in its *best* possible light, all things considered, is very questionable. Without this crucial assumption, the argument is not valid. And I think that very few of those who rely on the argument from the internal point of view share Dworkin's view about interpretation in this respect. But then they must come up with an alternative argument to fill in the gap.

Perhaps the following idea might help. In a very influential article, the philosopher W. B. Gallie suggested that there are certain concepts—such as democracy, art, or justice—that he called *essentially contested*, whereby people tend to have competing conceptions of the concept they share. Suppose it could be argued that "law," like democracy or art, is an *essentially contested concept*. Participants rationalize their normative attitude to law and their reasons for following legal rules on the basis of different and competing conceptions of the concept of law. This would make sense if the concept of law were an essentially contested concept, more or less along the lines suggested by Gallie's analysis.[33] Would it not then follow that any account of the internal point of view is normative, just as any theory of justice, or theory of democracy, must be normative? Such theories purport to defend a particular conception of a contested concept, and one that inevitably competes with other normative conceptions.

In order to assess such an argument, it is worth reminding ourselves what essentially contested concepts are. According to Gallie, there are five conditions: (1) The concept must be "appraisive," in that it stands for some kind of valued achievement. (2) This achievement must be internally complex, and (3) any explanation of its worth must refer to the respective contributions of its various parts or features. (4) The accredited achievement must be of a kind that admits of modifications in light of changing circumstances. And, finally, (5) each party recognizes the fact that its own understanding of the concept is contested by other parties.[34] Gallie's examples of essentially contested concepts include such things as democracy, art, social justice, and something like "the Christian way of life." Can we include the concept of law in this group?

I think not, because it is far from clear that law, in the relevant respect, is an "appraisive" concept in Gallie's sense. We must keep in mind that it is the concept of legal validity and the conditions of legal validity that form the focus of our interest. Legality, or legal validity, is basically a phase-sortal concept: Norms are either legally valid or not; they either belong to the law or they do not. Legal validity is not a kind of achievement that one can attain or fail to attain to a higher or lesser degree. Things can be more or less just, or more or less artistic, but this kind of appraisal is not something we can attribute to the validity of law. Of course, the enactment of *good* law is an achievement, and some laws are better than others—but surely not in terms of legal validity, per se. Good law is good because it promotes some good, not because it is more legal, or more law, as it were, than some alternative.

I do not wish to deny that one can fail to make law, or that there is some sense in which legality admits of degrees of success.

---

[33] Gallie, "Essentially Contested Concepts."
[34] Ibid., 171–80.

Many legal philosophers who have written about the rule of law (including myself) share the view that there are ways in which one can fail to make law.[35] There are certain conditions that the law has to meet in order to be able to fulfill its pivotal function of guiding human conduct. Law's ability, as a social instrument, to guide human conduct necessitates certain features the law must possess in order to fulfill such a function, regardless of its specific contents. And then there is a sense in which success or failure in this respect is a matter of degree. But this is quite irrelevant to the argument from the internal point of view. First, even if there is a sense in which "legality" is a form of achievement, it does not, by itself, make it an essentially contested concept. Second, and more importantly, this is not the relevant sense of legality that concerns us. As we have seen, the debate between legal positivism and its opponents is mainly about the conditions of legal validity; it is mainly about the question of what the law is, and what it is that renders certain norms legally valid and others not. In this respect, "law" is not an appraisive concept and therefore not an essentially contested one.[36]

So what is it about the concept of law of which participants and theorists can have competing and essentially contested conceptions? I suggest that it is not the concept of law, but the idea of good law, or legitimate law, that is, in a sense, an essentially contested concept. In other words, from the perspective of the participants, the law should be legitimate and justified. The legitimacy of the law in our society is something we have very good reasons to care about. And then we may have, as we do, very different conceptions about what the moral-political conditions of legitimacy are and what would make various laws better or worse than others. But none of this shows that the concept of law is an essentially contested concept, even from the internal point of view.

To sum up: A theory about the nature of law must account for the internal point of view. It must explain the sense in which participants regard the law as reason for their actions and what are

---

[35] See my "The Rule of Law and Its Limits," and references there.
[36] For a similar argument, claiming that law is not an essentially contested concept, see Green, "The Political Content of Legal Theory," 16–20.

the kinds of purposes or values that would render such reasons intelligible. But this is still a form of understanding, not judgment. We can understand various forms of practical reasoning without forming any evaluative judgment about them. And if we do not need to form a judgment about such reasoning, then jurisprudence is still basically descriptive and morally neutral.

SUGGESTED FURTHER READINGS

Dickson, *Evaluation and Legal Theory*.
Dworkin, *Justice in Robes*.
Raz, "The Argument from Justice, or How Not to Reply to Legal Positivism," 313.
———, "Two Views on the Nature of the Theory of Law: A Partial Comparison," 1.
Waldron, *Law and Disagreement*.
———, "Legal and Political Philosophy," 352.

The Language of Law

THE IMPORTANT ROLE that philosophy of language plays in articulating certain aspects of law has been well recognized by H.L.A. Hart. Throughout his writings, Hart made it very clear that he sees an understanding of language as central to his method of understanding law.[1] Some critics have misunderstood this methodological perspective, alleging that what Hart was after is an ordinary-language analysis of the meaning of the word *law*. In fact, not only had he not been engaged in anything like a linguistic analysis of *law*, but Hart also explicitly denied that such an endeavor would be fruitful.[2] Philosophy of language is central to an understanding of law for a different reason. Law, as we have seen in previous chapters, consists of authoritative directives. The content of the law is tantamount to the content that is communicated by various legal authorities. Authorities communicate, of course, in a natural language. Therefore, an understanding of how linguistic communication works and, in particular, how much is actually determined by various semantic and pragmatic aspects of language, is central to an understanding of what law is.

This chapter focuses on the role of language in understanding the content of the law. The argument in the first section is motivated by unfinished business left over from chapter 4. As we saw there, Dworkin argues that grasping the content of law is

---

[1] See, e.g., his inaugural lecture published as "Definition and Theory in Jurisprudence," in Hart, *Essays in Jurisprudence and Philosophy*, chap. 1; and Hart, *The Concept of Law*, chap. 1.

[2] Hart, *The Concept of Law*, 204. The suggestion that Hart's theory aimed at a semantic analysis of "law" was put forward by Dworkin, *Law's Empire*, chap. 1.

always a matter of interpretation. Since, as he argues, interpretation is partly, but necessarily, an evaluative matter, understanding what the law prescribes is necessarily dependent on evaluative considerations. If this were correct, Dworkin would have been right to conclude that legal positivism is fundamentally flawed. But Dworkin's assumptions about the role of interpretation in understanding what the law says are questionable. Thus, one main purpose of the argument here is to show why it makes no sense to assume that interpretation is as ubiquitous as Dworkin's argument assumes. We will see that interpretation is only the *exception* to understanding what the law says, not the standard way of grasping its content. Another main purpose of this chapter is to explain why interpretation is called for, and when, and what makes legal content indeterminate in some cases. Needless to say, these two arguments are connected. The better we understand the particular sources of indeterminacy of law, the better we understand the scope of its determinacy.

Do We Always Interpret the Law?

After a week or two of classes, first-year law students are rather surprised to learn how indeterminate and unclear the law is; they come to law school assuming that there is a body of knowledge about the law that they are going to learn, and that this knowledge is out there, written down in statutes and judicial decisions. By the end of first year in law school, students come to think that almost nothing is clear about the law, that it all depends on how courts interpret it, and that the best a lawyer can do is make an educated guess about what the relevant courts will do. They tend to think everything is up for grabs. But then, once they start working as lawyers in a firm, the picture reverses. Lawyers quickly learn that most of the litigation is not about the kinds of difficult legal issues they have studied in law school but about humdrum matters of fact—what has really happened, who said this or did that. And then they see that in the vast majority of the cases they handle disputes are settled out of court, and mostly because the law is clear enough; it is usually the facts the are in dispute.[3] Thus the truth is that both the laymen's picture of how determinate the law is, and the law students' impression of how indeterminate it is, are distorted. The law is much less clear than people tend to think, but it is much more clear than law students are led to believe, because they spend most of their studies focusing on the difficult or problematic cases that tend to reach the appellate courts.

The thesis under discussion here denies that this common-sense view—whereby in most cases it is clear enough what the law requires, and in other cases it calls for interpretation—is fundamentally mistaken. At a deeper level, some lawyers and philosophers claim, law is never clear; it is always a matter of interpretation to determine what the law actually says or requires. Let us begin by trying to understand what motivates such a view; why are some philosophers drawn to the idea that law is always subject to interpretation? After all, this view seems to fly in the face of our everyday experience. When we conduct an ordinary conversation, it is not our experience that every utterance by a speaker is somehow followed by a pause, when the hearer thinks about ways to interpret what has been said. Under the normal circumstance of a conversation, we just hear the utterances and thereby understand what has been said. So what is it that motivates the counterintuitive view that interpretation is always called for, or that interpretation is somehow always in the background?

I think that two kinds of motivation are in play. One stems from some general and familiar points about linguistic communication, and the other stems from certain unique features of law. Let me take up these two points in turn. It is a very familiar aspect of natural language that the content communicated by a speaker is often partly determined by certain contextual and normative factors. These contextual and normative determinates of linguistic contents are called the *pragmatic* aspects of language. In other words, it is a well-recognized fact that semantics and syntax (meaning) are essential vehicles for conveying communicative content, but the content that is actually communicated is often

---

[3] Of course, out-of-court settlement is sometimes induced by the fact that litigation would be too expensive to clarify a point of law.

partly determined by various pragmatic factors. Let us distinguish between the role that contextual knowledge plays and the role of a normative framework, and see whether either of these warrant the conclusion that interpretation is ubiquitous.

Knowledge of the relevant context often plays a crucial role in grasping the content that a speaker communicates. The most obvious examples concern the use of first-person pronoun *I*, indexical words such as *today* and *over here*, and demonstratives such as *he* and *they*. When we use such expressions in an utterance, it is obvious that the content communicated is partly determined by the meaning of the words we use and partly by certain facts that must be commonly known by speaker and hearer—such as who is speaking or which way one is pointing. But these are not the only cases. Consider, for example, the sentence, "I'm sorry but you are going to die." Now suppose that this sentence is uttered by a doctor examining a gunshot wound of a patient in the emergency room; and compare the same sentence uttered by a philosopher in response to a friend wondering why he should bother to do anything with his life. In the first context, the utterance is really bad news for the hearer. In the second context, not so; it is just a trite reminder of the fact that life is short, or something like that. Very different kinds of content might be conveyed by the same utterance, depending on the context of the conversation. Examples like this are abundant.

It would be wrong, however, if one concluded from such examples that understanding a linguistic expression necessarily involves interpretation. First, the fact that context often affects the content of speech does not entail that communicated content is always context sensitive. That would be a mistake of generalizing from some cases to all. Second, and more importantly, context sensitivity of communicated content does not entail that in understanding such expressions the hearer is necessarily engaged in anything we can call interpretation.[4] In most ordinary

---

[4] It is possible to stipulate that *interpretation* just stands for whatever mental processes are involved in grasping the meaning of an expression. In some linguistics literature, the word is used in that way. But this, of course, would not be the kind of concept of interpretation that Dworkin's argument assumes; there would not be anything necessarily evaluative, or even self-conscious, about it.

cases, the context of conversation is *common knowledge*, shared by speaker and hearer, and thus enables the hearer to grasp the relevant content without any particular difficulty or need for interpretation. Imagine the unfortunate gunshot-wounded patient in the ER being told by his doctor that he is going to die; I assume that questions of interpretation about what the doctor has just told him are not very likely to be the first thing that comes to his mind. In other words, the context dependence of our ability to communicate does not prove that interpretation somehow necessarily mediates between the meaning of the words and sentences uttered by a speaker and the hearer's grasp of the content communicated. For one thing, interpretation would be just as context dependent as any other aspect of linguistic communication. But the essential point is this: Communication is generally rendered possible because its context is typically common knowledge between the relevant parties to the conversation. Interpretation might be called for either because some particular aspect of the contextual background happens not to be sufficiently clear, or because in spite of the shared contextual background some aspect of the content conveyed remains unclear or indeterminate. But these must be the exceptional cases. Unless parties to a conversation could normally share the knowledge of the relevant context, linguistic communication would rarely succeed.

The role of a normative framework that must be presumed in any communicative context has been articulated by Paul Grice in his important work on pragmatic aspects of speech.[5] The basic idea is this: In an ordinary conversation, the relevant parties are normally engaged in a cooperative exchange of information. And this general purpose of a cooperative exchange of information entails that parties to a conversation must follow certain norms (or "maxims," as Grice called them). For example, a speaker must be presumed to have uttered something because he deems it relevant to the conversation and believes it to be true; the utterance has to be such that it does not say too little, or too much, in the context of the conversation; and it must be an orderly contribution, aiming to avoid obscurity, ambiguity, and such.

[5] Grice, *Studies in the Way of Words*.

These maxims are norms that directly instantiate the specific functions and purposes of communicative interactions and facilitate those purposes. Be relevant, truthful, do not say too little or too much, and the like, are maxims that apply to ordinary conversations because the purpose of the conversation is the cooperative exchange of information. Not all communicative interactions are of this nature, of course. We do not always engage in a cooperative exchange of information. And then, in other contexts, other norms may apply. In fact, we will see that in the legal context sometimes this normative framework is problematic. But for now, the essential point to keep in mind is that every communicative interaction is guided by some norms that govern the kind of contribution to the conversation that speakers are supposed to make. Without such a normative framework, typically shared by the relevant conversational parties, communication would not be possible.

Does this essential normative aspect of communication entail that every instance of speech is subject to interpretation? One might be tempted to reach such a conclusion if one assumes that the maxims of conversation are up for grabs, allowing the parties to a communicative interaction to have different understandings of the relevant norms that govern the conversation. But this would normally make no sense. I use the word *normally* purposefully here. It is always possible to have deviant cases; one may pretend to engage in an ordinary conversation, act manipulatively, or fail to follow the norms for various reasons. Furthermore, we will see that there are certain forms of strategic communication where the conversational maxims are somewhat uncertain. But this is still a far cry from the assumption that conversational maxims are always up for grabs, necessarily subject to interpretation. Without some shared normative background—at least a tacit mutual understanding of the maxims governing the conversation—parties to a conversation could not possibly engage in a communicative interaction.

We can see this very clearly when some aspect of this normative framework is misunderstood by one of the parties. Consider those cases when a speaker needs to clarify that she was misunderstood in this respect. "I was just kidding," the speaker says, for example, when the hearer must have understood her contribution

141

to the conversation to follow the regular maxims governing an ordinary exchange of information, when in fact it was meant as a joke. Or vice versa, sometimes the speaker needs to clarify that "I'm not kidding, it's true," to indicate that the conversation is back on the track of an ordinary informative conversation, not a humorous one.

To conclude this last point: Our ability to understand each other in a communicative context depends on a shared, at least tacit, understanding about the kind of conversation we are engaged in, and the norms governing it. Understandings of this kind are, of course, subject to occasional misunderstandings or deviations of various kinds, in which case, typically some aspect of the communication fails. None of this, however, is a matter of interpretation. From the fact that there is some normative framework governing the kind of conversation one is engaged in, it does not follow that a hearer's grasp of the communicative content hangs in the air, as it were, until she comes up with an interpretation of the relevant maxims. Maxims are typically *common knowledge* between speaker and hearer, in no need of interpretation.

We must look at another possibility of grounding the ubiquity of interpretation thesis. Perhaps it does not follow from general aspects of linguistic communication but from some unique aspects of the legal domain. Maybe there are some special features of law that make it the case that interpretation is always called for. The idea is not without some merit. If you think about the realm of arts, you might get an idea of why that might be the case. There is something about the nature of art that makes it very plausible to assume that an understanding of a work of art is, indeed, typically a matter of interpretation. The creation of a work of art is a form of communication but not of an informative kind. So what makes it the case that in understanding a work of art, or some aspect of it, one is typically engaged in interpretation? And is it the case that similar considerations apply to law as well?

The truth is that we do not need to provide a deep philosophical account here to explain what makes works of art subject to interpretation by their very nature. What we need is to see the relevant difference between art and law in this respect. And the difference is quite obvious: Works of art are created with an intention to be subject to different possible, potentially conflicting, interpretations. It is part of the concept of art, at least in our culture, that works of art are meant to be cultural objects that people can understand differently—relate to them in different, possibly conflicting and incompatible, ways. A work of art is not intended to convey a determinate communicative content that can simply be understood (or misunderstood); it is created with an intention to be somewhat indeterminate in content, or ambiguous in various ways, open to various interpretations.[6] None of this, however, applies to law. In fact, art and law could not be less similar in this respect. Legal instructions are meant to generate concrete results, providing people with particular reasons for action, thus aiming to affect our conduct in some specified ways. The level of specification may vary, of course; some laws are very specific, instructing specific modes of conduct or avoidance of them, while others are much more general. And then, the more general the legal norm is, the more likely it is that circumstances will arise where interpretation is called for. But, generally speaking, it is not in the nature of law, as it is in the nature of art, to become a cultural object that is detached from the specific communicative content it is meant to convey. Art is there to be interpreted; law is there to be acted upon.

Are there some other features unique to law that would make it the case that interpretation is always called for? An important institutional aspect of legal practice may give that impression. In every legal system, some agents enact laws, while some other agents are entrusted with determining how to apply the enacted norms to particular cases. As I have mentioned in chapter 1, there is a sense in which it is true that this determination of what the law means in particular cases, usually decided by courts or other judicial agencies, is the true or real content of the law.[7] In other

---

[6] This may not be the only reason for the ubiquity of interpretation in the realm of arts. The fact that art tends to communicate by employing various layers of symbolism and metaphor may also play a role. And there might be additional reasons.

[7] This is much more true about common law legal systems than about continental legal systems, where the doctrine of binding precedent is not recognized, at least not to the extent it is followed in common law.

words, it is typically the courts that get to determine what the law means or requires in particular cases of its application. And then, the familiar idea is that a court can understand or interpret the law any way it likes; and even after it determines how the law is to be applied or interpreted, a higher court, or the same court at some later time, may change its ruling and decide differently. Does not this show that law is always subject to interpretation?

The simple answer is no—it only shows that courts, especially higher courts, often have the legal power to modify the law by their judicial decisions. Let me explain briefly. Suppose that the following case arises: A statute prescribes that "all Xs who are F ought to φ," and suppose that a particular individual, A, is clearly and undoubtedly an F. Therefore, barring other potentially conflicting laws, A ought to φ. Now suppose that a court decides otherwise; it rules that, under the circumstances, it is not the case that A ought to φ. What are we to make of this? There are two possibilities: Either this court has made a legal error, transgressing its legal powers, in which case the law remains that A ought to φ, though perhaps this law will not be applied; or else the court has acted within its legal powers, in which case it simply modified the law. The law is now modified to prescribe that "All Xs who are F ought to φ, unless X is an A (or of type A, or something to that effect)." In most legal systems, such power to modify the law is reserved for the higher courts. But this is an institutional issue, which may vary from jurisdiction to jurisdiction. Generally speaking, however, courts can often change the law even when it is perfectly clear what the law, prior to their decision, was.[8]

To conclude this section: The commonsense view that the content of the law is often clear enough—and at other times, it is not—is the correct one. Mostly, just like in an ordinary conversation, we hear (or read, actually) what the legal directive says and thereby understand what it requires. In some cases, it is

---

[8] Part of what makes this obvious truth resistible or inconvenient is the fact that, in such cases, the court's modification of the law is bound to have a retroactive effect. This is obviously problematic, but probably unavoidable. I have explained this in greater detail in my "The Rule of Law and Its Limits."

unclear what the law says, and interpretation is called for. In the next section, I will discuss some of the main reasons for the need of interpretation in the law. I hope that if we understand what gives rise to the need for interpretation in the law, we will also get a better sense of what is determinate enough and in no need of interpretation.

WHY INTERPRET?

The law requires interpretation when its content is indeterminate in a particular case of its application. There are three main sources of indeterminacy in the law: conflict between different legal norms that apply, semantic indeterminacy, and some pragmatic features of communication. Note, however, that there is a distinction to be drawn between two types of cases. Sometimes, as noted in previous chapters, there is no law that applies to a particular case at hand. A particular dispute or legal question may be unsettled by existing law simply because there is no relevant law that applies. In such cases, courts need to settle the case by filling in the gap—by basically enacting the law that would decide the case. Whether we want to call such cases *interpretation* or not matters very little. The kinds of cases I will discuss, however, are those in which there is a relevant law that applies, but, for some reason, it is not entirely clear how it applies or what exactly it is that the law prescribes. In what follows I will try to explain the main reasons for such indeterminacies and, as I said, they are mostly of three kinds: reasons that derive from conflict of laws, from indeterminacy of the meaning of words and sentences in a natural language, and from some pragmatic features of communication.

Conflict of Laws

Given the sheer size of the law in a modern legal system and the vast number of legal norms that we have, it often happens that a particular case at hand is covered by more than one applicable legal norm. And it may happen that the legal norms that apply entail conflicting results. The typical cases are of the following structure; suppose there are two legal norms—

(1) "All Xs who are F ought to φ in circumstances C."
(2) "All Xs who are G ought to not-φ in circumstances C."

Now suppose that there is a particular individual, A, who happens to be both an F and a G. According to (1), in circumstances C, A ought to φ; according to (2), in circumstances C, A ought to not-φ. Surely, an A cannot both φ and not-φ under the same circumstances. Now, there are two possibilities. Sometimes there is a third legal norm that determines which one of the conflicting norms, (1) or (2), prevails under the circumstances. Thus, there may be a legal norm saying, in effect, that—

(3) In cases of conflict between (1) and (2), law (1) prevails.[9]

In this case, the conflict between the results entailed by (1) and (2) is not a real legal conflict, only an apparent one, since (3) determines a concrete result—that A ought to φ. Many times, however, no such hierarchy is determined by existing law. In other words, there is no norm of type (3). In such cases, the conflict between (1) and (2), with respect to the question of whether A ought to φ or not, is a genuine conflict—one for courts, presumably, to figure out. Now, of course, this is just a simple model. Conflicting results between different legal norms are often due to much more complex structures and, in some cases, it may not even be so clear that a conflict exists. My point here was very limited—only to point out that conflict between different legal norms that apply to a particular case is one major source for the need of interpretation in the law.

Semantic Indeterminacies

Laws are expressed in a natural language. The meaning of words and sentences in a natural language is often indeterminate with

---

[9] A simple example of this in U.S. law is the general norm that determines the supremacy of federal legislation over state legislation. Thus, if there is a conflict between federal law and state law, within certain boundaries prescribed by the U.S. Constitution, federal law prevails.

respect to its application to specific cases. The two central cases are ambiguity[10] and vagueness. Ambiguity might be generated either by the fact that a particular word or expression in a natural language happens to have two different meanings (such as the word *bank* in English, meaning either a financial institution or the side of a river), or else by the syntactical structure of a sentence (such as the sentence "I know a man with a dog who has fleas"; who has fleas—the man or the dog?). Ambiguity is typically resolved by knowledge of the relevant context of the utterance; given the context, we can normally tell which one of the two possible meanings is relevant under the circumstances. If you tell your friend that you are going to meet him at the bank while fishing in the river, presumably your friend will understand that it is not a financial institution you had in mind, but the bank of the river. And, vice versa, if you say this in the city while running some errands, it is very unlikely that your friend will aim to meet you at the bank of a nearby river. There is nothing to prevent the law from employing expressions that are ambiguous, either semantically or syntactically. Sometimes it may be very clear, from the context of the law, which one of the meanings is the relevant one, but there may be cases in which it is not so clear.

A much more prevalent source of indeterminacy in the law stems from the ubiquitous vagueness of words in a natural language. Most words in a natural language are vague. Vagueness consists in the fact that the application of the word to particular instances—called the word's extension—is bound to have some borderline cases, that is, cases in which it is indeterminate whether the word applies or not. Consider, for example a color word like *blue*. Some color perceptions are within the *definite extension* of *blue*, that is, they are undoubtedly blue, if anything is. Countless other color perceptions are within the *definite non-extension* of *blue*, that is, they are clearly and undoubtedly not blue, like red or yellow, and such. However, there is a range of

[10] Philosophers of language would resist the idea that ambiguity involves indeterminacy; I am not claiming otherwise. What is indeterminate in the case of ambiguity in law is the question of which meaning is legally relevant. Syntactical ambiguities, in particular, sometimes create a clear case of indeterminacy in the legal context.

borderline cases that may or may not be blue, that is, it would not be a mistake to call them *blue* and it would not be a mistake to call them *not blue*.[11] And the same goes for such borderline cases as the question of whether a person who is six feet high is "tall" or not, whether a person with a few dozen strings of hair is "bald," whether a large pamphlet is a "book," or whether a roller skate is a "vehicle."

It should not be difficult to see how vagueness generates indeterminacy in the law. In fact, I would venture to guess that most cases of statutory interpretation that courts tend to deal with concern borderline cases of vague terms in the relevant statute. It has become a jurisprudential tradition to use Hart's famous example of the ordinance prescribing "No vehicles allowed in the park," so let me stick to tradition and use this example. Clearly, the word *vehicle* has some definite extension: My Land Rover, quite new and in perfect working order, is a *vehicle,* if anything is. And it is equally clear that countless other objects are within the definite nonextension of *vehicle,* such as a doll carried by my daughter, or the sandwich I intend to consume in the park. However, there are borderline cases: Does this ordinance prohibit riding a bicycle in the park? And what about roller skates or motorized wheelchairs?

You might think that the law can avoid such indeterminacies simply by defining the general terms it employs. In our case, the law could add, for example, a statutory definition stipulating that, for purposes of this ordinance, *vehicle* includes bicycles but excludes roller skates and wheelchairs. True, the law can, and often does, provide such stipulations. Vagueness in the law can sometimes be reduced by such definitions and further clarifications. But it cannot be eliminated, or even reduced very substantially. First, there is a limit to how much detail any law can stipulate. Second, there is a limit to how many questions and problems legislatures can anticipate in advance. Third, and most importantly, vagueness cannot be eliminated because the words used in any definition are likely to be vague as well and would have borderline cases. So now we know, for example, that bicycles are within the extension of *vehicle* for the purposes of this ordinance, and then we would have borderline cases of what *bicycles* are. Think about

[11] See, for example, Soames, *Understanding Truth*, chap. 7.

children's tricycles, monocycles, and all sorts of contraptions that may rightly be called bicycles just as one may deny that they are bicycles.[12] Borderline cases there will always be.

Keep in mind, however, that borderline cases are just that, borderline cases. Even the vaguest of terms used in a law would have a definite extension of cases about which the relevant terms clearly and undoubtedly apply. However, in his famous debate with H.L.A. Hart, Lon Fuller argued that such linguistic considerations do not necessarily settle the legal issue.[13] Even if a particular legal case is such that it falls within the definite extension of the language of a legal rule, it may still be an open question whether the rule applies or not. An answer to the question of whether or how to apply the rule, Fuller argued, is always a matter of first determining the rule's purposes, and only in light of such a conception of what the rule is there for—what it aims to achieve—can we determine whether it applies to a particular case or not.

I find Fuller's argument unconvincing. His main example, which should give us a sense of what he had in mind, concerns the ordinance about vehicles in the park we have been using; what if a group of veterans, he asks, want to mount on a pedestal in the park a truck from World War II, which happens to be in working order? Still, it would be a memorial and, although a truck is certainly a vehicle, the prohibition of the ordinance should not apply, he suggests, because it was not the purpose of the rule to prohibit such memorials. What are we to make of this? I doubt that, as a matter of law, Fuller made a valid point here. If the veterans consulted an attorney, she would probably have told them to go ahead and seek an official permit before they start rolling the truck into the park. But even if I am wrong about this, I think that these kinds of cases rely on the phenomenon mentioned earlier, of conflict of norms. If the veterans' truck is, indeed, a case in which a truck (in working order) is not a *vehicle* for the purposes of a given rule, it is because there are other legal norms that conflict with it and call for a different outcome. More generally, the

[12] If you doubt that there are borderline cases of "bicycle," you may want to take a stroll on the Venice Beach bike path in Los Angeles; you will then see that there are all sorts of weird borderline cases of "bicycle" (and of many other things as well).

[13] Fuller, "Positivism and Fidelity to Law: A Reply to Professor Hart."

very idea that we cannot grasp the content of a rule and apply it to particular cases without first having some views about the rule's purposes seems implausible on its face. There are countless rules and conventions people follow without having much of an idea about the rules' purposes. Just think of the numerous social conventions we follow on a daily basis; I venture to guess that most of us have a very sketchy idea, at best, what the point of them is. But we follow them and certainly know how to apply them. Or, to take another example, if my dean requires that I provide a monthly report on the novels I read, I think that I will have a pretty good sense of what the rule requires, even if I would have no clue as to why he had made this rule or what the point of it is. Acquiring a view about the rule's purpose is certainly the sensible thing to do when you face a borderline case, and a decision is needed on how to classify it. This is usually how courts try to make their decisions about borderline cases.

Pragmatic Indeterminacies

The content that is communicated on an occasion of speech is not confined to content that is determined by the meaning of the words and sentences uttered by the speaker. Let us distinguish between two additional types of content. First, sometimes, what a speaker *says* or *asserts*—the content of the proposition that is conveyed—differs from the meaning of the words the speaker uttered. If I ask my wife when she gets home in the evening, "Have you eaten?" I am not asking her whether she has ever engaged in the activity of eating. I know that she has. The content that I assert here is obviously different—asking whether she has already had dinner that evening. And of course she would not have a particular difficulty in figuring this out. Generally, a speaker would normally succeed in conveying assertive content that differs from what she says when it would be obvious to the hearer, in the particular context of the utterance, that it just cannot be the case that the speaker asserts exactly what she says.

Does it happen in the legal context that the law asserts something different from what it says? It could happen, but not very frequently. First, lawmakers would certainly try to avoid this since it would be too easy to misunderstand what they meant. Second, in the legal context, we would normally lack sufficiently rich contextual background to enable the conclusion that what the law asserts is obviously not what it says. Consider, once again, the "no vehicles are allowed in the park" rule. Suppose, for example, that the legislature of this rule had taken it for granted that only motor vehicles are meant here and that is the content it intended to assert. One can imagine some circumstances in which it would be obvious that this is the case, but those would have to be pretty special circumstances, knowledge of which is shared by all parties concerned. We can imagine, for example, that the "no vehicles in the park" is enacted as a response to specific complaints about pollution, that this is known to be the case, and maybe forms part of a larger legislative measure that curbs motor vehicle pollution—then, yes, perhaps it is obvious that the ordinance is confined to motor vehicles. Otherwise, it is likely to remain an open question.[14]

The second and much more prevalent type of cases concerns those in which the content communicated by a speaker goes beyond what the speaker asserted. In many familiar cases, some communicative content is implied, though not quite asserted, by the speaker in the particular context of his utterance. Consider, for example, a municipal ordinance requiring restaurants to have "clean and well-maintained bathrooms indoors." Even if the regulation does not explicitly mention this, surely we would assume that a restaurant that had impeccable bathrooms that are kept locked at all times would violate the ordinance. That the restrooms need to be open for patrons to use is content that is clearly implicated by such an ordinance.

Generally, the implied content of the utterance of *P* in context *C* can be defined as the content that the speaker, in the specific context of *C*, is *committed to* by uttering *P*, and the hearers are expected to know that the speaker is committed to, and the speaker can be expected to know this. A speaker can be expected to be

---

[14] The famous case of *Holy Trinity Church v. United States*, 143 U.S. 457 (1892), exemplifies how problematic this is; I elaborated on these problems in my "The Pragmatics of Legal Language."

committed to such implied content if and only if an explicit, ex post facto denial of the implied content would strike any reasonable hearer under the circumstances as perplexing, disingenuous, or contradictory. There are several kinds of implied content. I will concentrate here on one familiar category, identified and explained by Grice, called conversational implicatures.

To mention another example, given by Grice, consider the following situation: *X*, standing near his immobilized car that ran out of gas, asks for the help of *Y*, a local person passing by. Knowing these facts, *Y* says, "There is a gas station in the next village." Now, *Y* has not actually *asserted* that (for all he knows) the gas station is open and would have gas to sell. But given the maxims of conversation (for example, be relevant, do not say something you believe to be false, and such), it would be natural to assume that this content was implicated by what *Y* has said. It is content that *Y* is committed to, given the situation and the conversational maxims that apply.[15]

Thus, to define more generally, a speaker *S* conversationally implicates *q* by saying *p* in context *C*, if—

    (a) *S* is presumed to observe the relevant conversational maxims in *C*;

    (b) the assumption that *S* meant (or intended that) *q* is required in order to make sense of *S*'s utterance of *p* in context *C*, given the conversational maxims that apply;

    (c) *S* believes/assumes that his/her hearers can recognize condition *b*, and can recognize that *S* knows that.[16]

As Grice emphasized, there are two main features essentially associated with conversational implicatures:

    (1) Conversational implicatures are always *cancelable* by the speaker. The speaker in our example could have added, "but I'm not sure that the gas station is open," in which

---

[15] Grice, *Studies in the Way of Words*, 32.

[16] This last condition of transparency is actually rather problematic and controversial. Grice himself was aware of a serious problem here considering the implicatures involved in using disjunction. See Soames, "Drawing the Line between Meaning and Implicature—and Relating Both to Assertion."

case the implicature would be explicitly canceled. Generally speaking, cancelability is an essential feature of conversational implicatures.

(2) Conversational implicatures are very context specific; they are not conventionally determined by the rules of language. There is always some derivation, as Grice called it, that leads us to construe the content of an implicature; some story has to be known or to be assumed to make it explicit.[17]

Let us now return to law. In the legal context, implicatures are certainly a potential source of indeterminacy. In some contexts, implicatures cannot be ignored; our earlier example of the ordinance requiring restaurants to maintain bathrooms is a case in point. At other times, however, implicatures tend to be ignored by the courts, even if their content is clear. Here is a familiar example: Countless laws assert something in the form of a general norm with some explicit exceptions: "All Xs ought to φ unless X is an F, a G, or an H." (Or, which is the more typical case, the law asserts that "all Xs ought to φ," followed by another section prescribing an explicit exemption to those who are F, G, or H.) This kind of utterance would normally implicate that the mentioned exceptions are exhaustive—that *all* Xs who are not (F or G or H) ought to φ. Note that this implicature is cancelable; the legislature can easily indicate that it does not consider the exceptions to be exhaustive. However, absent such indication, it would be natural to assume that the legislature has implicated that F, G, and H are the only permissible exceptions to the requirement of Xs to φ.

Every first-year law student learns, however, that courts are not very consistent in applying such implicatures. Judges tend to be rather skeptical, and perhaps rightly so, of the legislature's ability to determine in advance all the possible justified exceptions to rules it enacts. Sometimes, therefore, courts simply ignore the implicature; they treat a list of exceptions as suggestive rather than

---

[17] This second condition should be qualified, however; Grice also identified a category of cases he called "generalized conversational implicatures," in which the implication is less context dependent, partly deriving from the meaning of the words uttered. See Grice, *Studies in the Way of Words*, 37–40.

exhaustive.[18] In such cases, the courts are basically hearing, so to speak, the assertive content of the legislative speech while ignoring the communicative content that was not quite asserted but only implicated by it.

Why is it really a case of indeterminacy as opposed to one in which the courts simply fail to follow the law? The answer stems from the fact that legislation is not an ordinary conversation; the conversation between the legislature and the courts, so to speak, is not one of a cooperative exchange of information. It is, partly, a strategic form of communication, and one in which the maxims of conversation are not entirely determined and/or certain. In other words, the source of indeterminacy derives from the nature of the conversation, not merely from the distinction between asserted and implicated content. Let me try to explain this in some detail.

The enactment of a law is not a cooperative exchange of information. Legislation is typically a form of *strategic behavior*. In fact, the situation is more complicated because legislation consists of several conversations, not one. There is a conversation between the legislators themselves during the enactment process, and then the result of this internal conversation is another conversation between the legislature and the courts (or various agencies).[19] The internal conversation is, more often than not, very strategic in nature. It certainly does not abide by the Gricean maxims of a cooperative exchange of information. And then, when courts and others look at the result of this internal conversation within the legislature, it would be difficult to ignore its strategic nature that generated the collective speech.

The most familiar aspect of legislation is that it is almost always a result of a compromise. Compromise often consists in what I would like to call *tacitly acknowledged incomplete decisions*, that

---

[18] A famous case in point is *Holy Trinity*; see my "The Pragmatics of Legal Language."

[19] I assume here that there is an ongoing conversation, as it were, between the legislature and the courts; the courts respond by ways in which they interpret the legislative language and various "doctrines" of statutory interpretation that they proclaim.

is, decisions that deliberately leave certain issues undecided.[20] This is closely tied to the problem of collective agency:

> X would want to say that "P" intending to implicate Q.
> Y would want to say that "P" intending to implicate not-Q.
> X and Y act collectively, <u>intending</u> *their collective speech in saying* P *to remain undecided about the implication of* Q.

The general problem is that the underlined *intending* is often not so clear; in fact, the typical case would be one of conflicting and incompatible intentions, hopes, expectations, and such, namely, both X and Y intending—or hoping or expecting—their intentions to prevail. In some cases, this may not be problematic. It is certainly possible that both X and Y would have conflicting intentions or expectations about the implication of Q without intending their *collective* speech to implicate anything about Q. But it would be unrealistic to assume that this is always, or even typically, the case. More often than not, legislators would like to have their legislative agenda realized in practice; they would want to achieve certain goals that are better served by an interpretation of the bill they enact in ways in which they hope or expect it to be understood. In other words, the typical case would be the one in which both X and Y expect or at least hope that the *collective expression of P* would implicate (or not) that Q.

When this kind of collective action involves numerous agents, sometimes hundreds of legislators, with different political agendas and expectations about bills they enact, the difficulties are evident. In Gricean terms, the problem in such cases is twofold. First, there is a considerable indeterminacy about *who* counts as a relevant party to the conversation—for example, the initiators of the bill, the less than enthusiastic supporters, those who voted against as well? And, second, there is an inherent uncertainty about *what* counts as a relevant contribution to the conversation that different parties are allowed to make.

Strategic behavior is not confined, however, to internal conversation among the legislators. Consider those cases, for example, in which the legislature deliberately speaks in several voices, as it

---

[20] There is nothing new in this idea; numerous writers have noted it.

were. There are legislative enactments in which the legislature intends to convey one message to the public at large and a different one to agencies or the courts. Meir Dan-Cohen has explained this phenomenon, and its rationale, in the context of criminal law.[21] To mention one of his examples, consider the defense of duress. This is a very problematic defense. On the one hand, considerations of deterrence weigh against recognizing such a defense; we would not want to encourage people to succumb to threats and commit crimes out of fear or weakness of character. On the other hand, considerations of fairness and human compassion call for recognition of such a defense. It would be very unfair to punish people for things they have done under enormous threat. This is a serious conflict, but one that allows a certain solution: The law could generate the impression that it does not recognize duress as a defense, or that it would only grant it in extremely dire circumstances, but, at the same time, the law could instruct the courts to grant the defense when considerations of fairness and compassion call for it. As Dan-Cohen demonstrates, this is more or less what actually happens in common law. And it makes a lot of sense.

I hope you can see that the temptation to use this device might be great in many legislative contexts. Legislators may wish to create the impression that they are doing one thing—for example, seriously restricting campaign finance contributions—while actually trying to do the opposite—allowing such contributions to flow freely but less transparently. What we have in such cases is almost like a conflicting implicature: Looked at from one angle, the legislature implicates one thing; looked at from a different angle, it implicates the opposite. Furthermore, as the two examples just mentioned show, there is no general policy that can apply across the board. In some cases, such as the example of duress, the legislative double-talk makes a lot of sense and is probably morally commendable. In other cases, such as the campaign finance example, the double-talk is rather questionable. Either way, I do not think that there is a clear answer to the question

---

[21] See Dan-Cohen, "Decision Rules and Conduct Rules: On Acoustic Separation in Criminal Law."

of what the unique content of the law is in such cases of double-talk. The same speech act implicates different content in different contexts, or for different audiences, even if the contents are mutually inconsistent.

Let me pause to take some stock. I have tried to show that unlike regular conversational contexts where the parties to the conversation aim at a cooperative exchange of information, a partly noncooperative form of communication is present in the legislative context. The process of legislation is plagued with strategic behavior that tries to overcome the lack of initial cooperation among the relevant agents. And then, once we have the result of this process, it becomes very difficult to determine which aspects of it are relevant to determining the content of the legislative speech, and which aspects ought to be ignored.

Much more needs to be explored about the ways in which strategic conversation works, and about the kinds of maxims that may or may not apply to such a unique normative framework. My own suspicion is that a certain level of uncertainty about the relevant maxims of conversation is essential to making strategic speech possible.[22] There is, however, one caveat that needs to be mentioned. Over time, the norms of statutory interpretation that are actually followed by the courts may partly determine some conversational maxims of legislation. In following certain norms about the ways in which courts interpret statutory language, the courts could create some kind of Gricean maxims for the legislative context. For example, the extent to which courts are willing to hear evidence about statutory history would partly determine the norms of relevance about legislative implication. These norms would partly determine what counts as a relevant contribution to the conversation between legislators and the courts, so to speak. Thus, to some extent, and greatly depending on the interpretative culture of the courts, some Gricean maxims might be present even in the legislative context. Note that the reliability of such norms crucially depends on the actual consistency, over time,

---

[22] I have argued for this conclusion in my "Can the Law Imply More Than It Says?" (forthcoming in Marmor and Soames, eds., *The Philosophical Foundations of Language in Law*).

of the interpretative practices of the courts. If the courts do not consistently adhere to the relevant interpretative practices, the legislators would not have clear signals about what would count as a relevant contribution to the conversation between them and the courts, and, therefore, inevitably, even among the legislators themselves. But again, if my suggestion about the uncertainty of norms of strategic conversation is correct, we should realize that neither the courts nor the legislature would necessarily have a very strong incentive to follow norms of interpretation very consistently.

Before we conclude this discussion, let me warn against too much skepticism; even with respect to implicated content, a great deal is determined by the rules of language. Not every kind of implicature is context sensitive. There are many cases in which a certain expression used by a speaker implicates a certain content simply due to the meaning of the expression used. In other words, some implications are *semantically encoded* in the expression that the speaker asserted. Grice called these "conventional implicatures."[23] Consider, for example, the following utterances:

(1) "Even A can φ" (implicating that there are some others, besides A, who can φ, and that A is one of the least likely among them to φ).

(2) "A managed to find X" (implicating that finding X was expected to involve some difficulty).

(3) "It was A who broke the vase" (implicating that somebody must have broken the vase).

In all these cases, and many others like them, the implicated content is semantically encoded in the utterance. And this is clearly manifested by the fact that the implied content is not cancelable by the speaker. It makes no sense to utter (3) and then try to cancel the implication by adding that nobody actually broke the vase. Similarly, it makes no sense to say something like (1) "Even John can pass the exam; after all, he is the best student." It is impossible to imagine any context in which such an utterance would make sense. Thus, semantically encoded implications are

[23] Grice, *Studies in the Way of Words*, 24–26, 41, 46, 86.

not affected by the strategic nature of legal speech. If there is some content that is semantically implicated by the formulation of a legal directive, it would normally form part of the content that is actually determined by the law.

SUGGESTED FURTHER READINGS

Endicott, *Vagueness in Law*.
Marmor, "The Pragmatics of Legal Language," 423.
Marmor and Soames, eds., *The Philosophical Foundations of Language in the Law*.
Moore, "The Semantics of Judging."
Soames, *Philosophical Essays*, vol. 1, chaps. 10, 11, and 15.
Stavropoulos, "Hart's Semantics," 59.

Bibliography

Arneson, Richard. "Democracy Is Not Intrinsically Just." In *Justice and Democracy*, edited by K. Dowding and R. E. Goodin. Cambridge: Cambridge University Press, 2004, 40.

Austin, John. *The Province of Jurisprudence Determined*. London: J. Murray, 1832.

Bentham, Jeremy. *An Introduction to the Principles of Morals and Legislation*. A reprint of the edition of 1823, which contains the author's final collections. New York: Hafner, 1948.

Campbell, Tom. *The Legal Theory of Ethical Positivism*. Brookfield, VT; Aldershot, UK: Dartmouth, 1996.

Cohen, Marshall, ed. *Ronald Dworkin and Contemporary Jurisprudence*. London: Duckworth; Totowa, NJ: Rowman and Allanheld, 1984, 28.

Coleman, Jules. "Negative and Positive Positivism." *Journal of Legal Studies* 11, no. 1 (1982): 139–64.

———. *The Practice of Principle*. New York: Oxford University Press, 2001.

Coleman, Jules, ed. *Hart's Postscript: Essays on the Postscript to The Concept of Law*. Oxford: Oxford University Press, 2001.

Dan-Cohen, Meir. "Decision Rules and Conduct Rules: On Acoustic Separation in Criminal Law." In *Harmful Thoughts*, 37. Princeton, NJ: Princeton University Press, 2002.

Darwall, Stephen. "Authority and Second-Personal Reasons for Acting." In *Reasons for Action*, edited by D. Sobel and S. Wall, 134. Cambridge: Cambridge University Press, 2009.

Dickson, Julie. *Evaluation and Legal Theory*. Oxford: Hart Publishing, 2001.

Dworkin, Ronald. *Justice in Robes*. Cambridge, MA: Belknap Press of Harvard University Press, 2006.

———. *Law's Empire*. Cambridge, MA: Belknap Press of Harvard University Press, 1986.

———. *Taking Rights Seriously*. London: Duckworth, 1977.

Elster, Jon. *Ulysses Unbound*. Cambridge: Cambridge University Press, 2000.

Endicott, Timothy A. O. *Vagueness in Law*. New York: Oxford University Press, 2001.

Finnis, John. *Natural Law and Natural Rights*. New York: Oxford University Press, 1980.

———. "On Reason and Authority in *Law's Empire*." *Law and Philosophy* 6, no. 3 (1987): 357.

Fuller, Lon. "Positivism and Fidelity to Law: A Reply to Professor Hart." *Harvard Law Review* 71 (1958): 630.

Gallie, W. B. "Essentially Contested Concepts." *Proceedings of the Aristotelian Society* (1956): 167.

Gardner, John. "Legal Positivism: 5 1/2 Myths." *American Journal of Jurisprudence* 46 (2001): 199–227.

Gavison, Ruth, ed. *Issues in Contemporary Legal Philosophy: The Influence of H.L.A. Hart*. Oxford: Clarendon Press, 1987.

George, Robert P., ed. *Natural Law Theory*. Oxford: Clarendon Press, 1992.

Green, Leslie. *The Authority of the State*. Oxford: Clarendon Press, 1990.

———. "The Concept of Law Revisited." *Michigan Law Review* 94 (1996): 1687.

———. "The Political Content of Legal Theory." *Philosophy of the Social Sciences* 17 (1987): 1–20.

———. "Positivism and Conventionalism." *Canadian Journal of Law and Jurisprudence* 12, no. 1 (1999): 35–52.

Grice, H. Paul. *Studies in the Way of Words*. Cambridge, MA: Harvard University Press, 1981.

Hart, H.L.A. *The Concept of Law*. 1st ed. Oxford: Clarendon Press, 1961.

———. *The Concept of Law*. 2nd ed., with a postscript edited by P. Bulloch and J. Raz. Oxford: Clarendon Press, 1994.

———. *Essays in Jurisprudence and Philosophy*. Oxford: Clarendon Press, 1983.

———. *Essays on Bentham*. Oxford: Clarendon Press, 1982.

Hartogh, Govert den. *Mutual Expectations: A Conventionalist Theory of Law*. New York: Kluwer Law International, 2002.

Himma, Kenneth. "Inclusive Legal Positivism." In *The Oxford Handbook of Jurisprudence and Philosophy of Law*, edited by J. Coleman, S. Shapiro, et al. New York: Oxford University Press, 2002.

Hobbes, Thomas. *Leviathan*. Edited by Edwin Curley. Cambridge: Hackett, 1994.

Hohfeld, W. N. *Fundamental Legal Conceptions*. Edited by W. W. Cook. New Haven, CT: Yale University Press, 1919.

Holmes, Oliver Wendell, Jr. "The Path of the Law." *Harvard Law Review* 10 (1897): 457.

Kelsen, Hans. *General Theory of Law and State*. Translated by A. Wedberg. 1945. New York: Russell and Russell, 1961.

―――. *Introduction to the Problems of Legal Theory*. Translated by B. L. Paulson and S. L. Paulson. A translation of *Reine Rechtslehre*, published in 1934. Oxford: Clarendon Press, 2002.

―――. *Pure Theory of Law*. 2nd ed. Translated by M. Knight. 1960. Berkeley: University of California Press, 1967.

Lagerspetz, Eerik. *The Opposite Mirrors: An Essay on the Conventionalist Theory of Institutions*. Dordrecht; Boston: Kluwer, 1995.

Leiter, Brian. "Legal Realism." In *Companion to Philosophy of Law and Legal Theory*, edited by D. Patterson, 261. Cambridge, MA: Blackwell, 1996.

―――. *Naturalizing Jurisprudence*. New York: Oxford University Press, 2007.

Lewis, David. *Convention: A Philosophical Study*. Oxford: Basil Blackwell, 1968.

Llewellyn, Karl N. *Jurisprudence: Realism in Theory and Practice*. New Brunswick, NJ: Transaction Publishers, 2008.

MacCormick, Neil. *H.L.A. Hart*. 2nd ed. Stanford, CA: Stanford University Press, 2008.

―――. "A Moralistic Case for A-Moralistic Law?" *Valparaiso Law Review* 20 (1985).

Marmor, Andrei. "Exclusive Legal Positivism." In *The Oxford Handbook of Jurisprudence and Philosophy of Law*, edited by J. Coleman, S. Shapiro, et al. New York: Oxford University Press, 2002.

―――. *Interpretation and Legal Theory*. 2nd ed. Oxford; Portland, OR: Hart Publishing, 2005.

―――. *Law in the Age of Pluralism*. New York: Oxford University Press, 2007.

―――. "Legal Positivism: Still Descriptive and Morally Neutral." *Oxford Journal of Legal Studies* 26 (2006): 683.

―――. "The Pragmatics of Legal Language." *Ratio Juris* 21 (2008): 423.

―――. "The Rule of Law and Its Limits." University of Southern California Law and Public Policy Research Paper No. 03-16. April 2003.

Bibliography

Marmor, Andrei. *Social Conventions: From Language to Law*. Princeton, NJ: Princeton University Press, 2009.

Marmor, Andrei, ed. *Law and Interpretation: Essays in Legal Philosophy*. Oxford: Clarendon Press, 1995.

Marmor, Andrei, and Scott Soames, eds., *The Philosophical Foundations of Language in the Law*. Oxford, forthcoming.

Moore, Michael. "The Semantics of Judging." *Southern California Law Review* 54 (1981): 151.

Perry, Stephen. "Hart's Methodological Positivism." In *Hart's Postscript: Essays on the Postscript to* The Concept of Law, edited by J. Coleman, 323. Oxford: Oxford University Press, 2001.

———. "Interpretation and Methodology in Legal Theory." In *Law and Interpretation*, edited by A. Marmor, 123. Oxford: Clarendon Press, 1995.

Postema, Gerald. *Bentham and the Common Law Tradition*. Oxford: Clarendon Press, 1989.

Raz, Joseph. "The Argument from Justice, or How Not to Reply to Legal Positivism." In *The Authority of Law*. 2nd ed. New York: Oxford University Press, 2009.

———. "Authority, Law, and Morality." *Monist* 68 (1985): 295.

———. *The Authority of Law*. Oxford: Clarendon Press, 1979.

———. *Between Authority and Interpretation*. New York: Oxford University Press, 2009.

———. *The Concept of a Legal System*. 1970. Oxford: Clarendon Press, 1980.

———. *Engaging Reason*. Oxford: Oxford University Press, 1999.

———. *Ethics in the Public Domain*. Oxford: Clarendon Press, 1994.

———. "Legal Principles and the Limits of Law." In *Ronald Dworkin and Contemporary Jurisprudence*, edited by M. Cohen, 73. London: Duckworth; Totowa, NJ: Rowman and Allanheld, 1984.

———. *The Morality of Freedom*. Oxford: Clarendon Press, 1986.

———. *Practical Reason and Norms*. 1975. Princeton, NJ: Princeton University Press, 1990.

———. "Two Views on the Nature of the Theory of Law: A Partial Comparison." In *Hart's Postscript: Essays on the Postscript to* The Concept of Law, edited by J. Coleman. Oxford: Oxford University Press, 2001.

Scanlon, Thomas. *What We Owe to Each Other*. Cambridge, MA: Belknap Press of Harvard University Press, 1998.

Schroeder, Mark. "Cudworth and Normative Explanations." *Journal of Ethics and Social Philosophy* 1, no. 3 (2005), at www.jesp.org.

Shapiro, Scott. "Authority." In *The Oxford Handbook of Jurisprudence and Philosophy of Law*, edited by J. Coleman, S. Shapiro, et al., 382. New York: Oxford University Press, 2002.

———. "On Hart's Way Out." In *Hart's Postscript: Essays on the Postscript to* The Concept of Law, edited by J. Coleman, 149. Oxford: Oxford University Press, 2001.

Soames, Scott. "Drawing the Line between Meaning and Implicature—and Relating Both to Assertion." In *Philosophical Essays*, vol. 1, 298–326. Princeton, NJ: Princeton University Press, 2009.

———. *Philosophical Essays*. Vol. 1. Princeton, NJ: Princeton University Press, 2009.

———. *Understanding Truth*. New York: Oxford University Press, 1999.

Stavropoulos, Nicos. "Hart's Semantics." In *Hart's Postscript: Essays on the Postscript to* The Concept of Law, edited by J. Coleman, 59. Oxford: Oxford University Press, 2001.

Waldron, Jeremy. *Law and Disagreement*. Oxford: Clarendon Press, 1999.

———. "Legal and Political Philosophy." In *The Oxford Handbook of Jurisprudence and Philosophy of Law*, edited by J. Coleman, S. Shapiro, et al. New York: Oxford University Press, 2002.

———. "Normative (or Ethical) Positivism." In *Hart's Postscript: Essays on the Postscript to* The Concept of Law, edited by J. Coleman, 410. Oxford: Oxford University Press, 2001.

Waluchow, Wilfrid. *Inclusive Legal Positivism*. Oxford: Clarendon Press, 1994.

Index

American legal realism, 30–33, 34
anarchism, 21, 22, 26
Augustine, St., 4
Austin, John, 12n1, 114n9; and commands, 35, 36–41; and Hart, 35, 47, 55, 57, 67; and morality, 109; and rules, 49; and rules of transition, 46–47; and sanctions, 44; and social rules, 54; and sovereignty, 44–45, 61
authoritative decisions, 92
authoritative directives: and language, 136; law as, 89; legal norms as, 60–61, 83
authority: and Austin, 45; and belief, 72; and coordination problems, 68, 80; and identity-related reasons for action, 68; and inclusive legal positivism, 96–97; legal constraints on, 67–69; legitimacy of, 58–59, 65, 66, 72–73; and normativity, 60–73; and obligation, 61–62, 63–67, 70, 71; and Raz, 8–9; and reduction, 73; and right to rule, 64, 65–66; self-binding, 67–69; and service, 64, 65, 66, 68; and social rules, 73

basic norm, 15–20; content of, 22; content of determined by practice, 25; defined, 16–17; and efficacy, 19–20, 22, 23; and Hart, 35, 51; and legal systems, 18; and legal validity, 20–21; presupposition of, 19, 20–21, 22, 48, 50, 51; reasons for endorsing, 72; and rules of recognition, 49–50; and social facts, 23–24, 25, 28; and social practice, 51; validity of, 22
Bentham, Jeremy, 39n6, 117

Campbell, Tom, 111, 113–14, 115
cases, unsettled, 84–85, 86, 87–88, 91
coercion: and Dworkin, 110, 120–21; legitimacy of, 110. See also force; sanctions
command/command theory of law, 35, 36–44, 49, 57, 61
common law tradition, 88
constitution, 69, 105
constitutional documents, 93
conventionalism, 9, 80, 111, 120–21
conventional rules: as arbitrary, 76–77; as compliance dependent, 76–77; defined, 77–78. See also rules
conventions, 73–83; authorities as constituted by, 83; and morality, 95; as normative solutions to coordination problems, 79; rules of recognition as, 95–96; and social rules, 60
coordination: and authority, 68, 80; and conflict of interest, 80n22; and conventions, 74, 76, 79; and morality, 124; as rationale for law, 80; and Raz, 42; and rules of recognition, 78, 79, 81, 82

Dan-Cohen, Meir, 156
detached normative statements, 26, 54
detachment, 10; and Dworkin, 9; of factual aspects from normative content, 7, 23; and Hart, 8, 9, 61; and Kelsen, 14; of law from sovereignty, 8, 61; of legal validity from evaluative content, 5; of legal validity from morality, 6, 7, 14, 92, 109, 110; and reduction, 8
Dickson, Julie, 125n25
directed power, 93–94

Index

Dworkin, Ronald, 5, 9, 122; constructive model of, 128; and conventionalism, 120–21; and evaluation, 128–30; and inclusive legal positivism, 95; and interpretation, 9, 97–108, 109–10, 122, 132, 136–37; *Law's Empire*, 111, 120; and legal conventionalism, 111; and legal error, 96–97; on legal rules vs. legal principles, 85–92; methodological argument of, 126, 127; and Raz, 96; and rules of recognition, 75–76, 77

enactment, of law, 15–17
enforcement, 39, 40
error, legal, 91, 92, 97
essentially contested concept, 132–33
ethical legal positivism, 111, 115–16, 121

factual aspects of law, and normative content, 7–8. *See also* social facts
Finnis, John, 5n4
force, 40, 41, 42. *See also* coercion; sanctions
Fuller, Lon, 149
function, of law: and coercion, 40, 41–42, 43, 44; and coordination, 43, 79, 80; as guiding human conduct, 134; and normativity, 119–20; and obligation vs. power-conferring, 38–39; and Perry, 122, 123–25; and rules of recognition, 78–79, 82; and secondary rules, 119

Gallie, W. B., 132–33
game, law as, 45–46
Green, Leslie, 80, 81
Grice, Paul, 140, 152–53, 154, 155, 157, 158

Hart, H. L. A., 60, 67, 70, 112, 123; and American legal realism, 31, 32; and Austin, 35, 47, 55, 57; and coercion, 43; and commands, 37, 38; and detachment view, 8, 9, 61; and Dworkin, 85; and Fuller, 149; and Hobbes, 41; and internal point of view, 123, 130, 131; and judicial discretion, 107; and Kelsen, 35, 39, 40–42, 54–55; and language, 136; and legal positivism, 75, 83, 110, 111; and legal principles, 88; and legal validity, 35, 116; and legal vs. moral obligations, 71; and morality, 58, 109, 111, 112, 116, 118, 122; and normativity, 35, 48, 119; and obligation, 57, 71–72; and political sovereignty, 61; and reduction, 8, 35, 51, 52, 53, 55, 73, 83; and sanctions, 41–42, 44; and social facts, 55, 71–72, 116; and social rules, 9, 35, 48–59; and sociology, 35, 55, 71; and sovereignty, 8, 41, 45, 46; and vagueness, 148
Hobbes, Thomas, 4n3, 8, 36, 41
Hohfeld, W. N., 37n3
Holmes, Oliver Wendell, Jr., "The Path of the Law," 30n26
Holy Trinity Church v. United States, 151n14
Hume, David, 17, 21, 23

implicature/implied content, 151–54, 158–59
inclusive legal positivism, 92–97
indeterminacy: and ambiguity, 147n10; and conflict of laws, 145–46; and interpretation, 137–38, 145; pragmatic, 150–59; semantic, 145, 146–50
institutions, 43; authoritative, 63; different types of, 41; and Raz, 42–43; rules as constituting, 47, 49–50; social, 113; sovereignty as, 47–48
intention, 99, 101–3, 104–5
internal point of view, 53–55, 123, 130–35
interpretation: all things considered, 132; ambiguity in, 127–28; and basic norm, 20–21; and best possible example/light, 98, 100, 101, 103, 105–7, 128, 132; constructive, 100, 101, 105;

and Dworkin, 9, 97–108, 109–10, 122, 136–37; and evaluation, 100, 107–8, 128–30; and indeterminacy, 137–38, 145; intention in, 99, 101–3, 104–5; and internal point of view, 130–35; by judges/courts, 137–38, 144, 145; and language, 9–10, 137–45; law as, 97–108; and legal validity, 29; and meaning, 29; and normativity, 29; and philosophy of law, 34, 109–10, 122, 126–30; as value laden, 127
is-ought problem, 17, 19, 23

judges/courts: and American legal realism, 30–33, 34; as constituted by the law, 31–32; and conventional rules, 78; and coordination, 79, 81; creation of law by, 2, 85, 89, 90, 91; and Dworkin, 75–76; and implicatures, 153–54; institutional role of, 90; interpretation by, 137–38, 144, 145; and legal positivism, 113, 114–15; and legislature, 154; and obligation to rules of recognition, 73, 82; rules as constituting role of, 56, 76; and rules of recognition, 51, 55–56, 58, 75–76, 81–82; and unsettled cases, 84–85, 86, 87–88. *See also* legal officials
judicial discretion, 84–92, 107
judicial rhetoric, 90
jurisdiction, 3, 19n11

Kant, Immanuel, 20, 21, 27
Kelsen, Hans, 8; and agenda-displacement theory, 33; and American legal realism, 33; and basic norm, 15–25, 50, 72; and Hart, 35, 39, 40–42, 54–55; and interpretation, 15–16; and legal validity, 35; and legal vs. moral obligations, 71; and morality, 13, 14, 21, 26, 71, 109; and natural law, 25–26, 27; and normativity, 25–27, 54–55; and obligation, 26;

and political sovereignty, 41; *Pure Theory of Law,* 23; and pure theory of law, 13–34; and Raz, 25, 26; and reduction, 8, 14, 15, 19, 20, 28–29, 30, 33, 35; and sanctions, 41, 44; and social facts, 72; and social practice, 19; and sociology, 14, 15

language, 136–59; ambiguity in, 147; and authoritative directives, 136; and context, 138–40, 150, 151, 157; and implied content, 151–54, 158–59; and interpretation, 9–10, 137–45; normative determinates of, 138–39; normative framework of, 140–42; pragmatic aspects of, 138–39; vagueness in, 147–49
legal officials, 33; and conventional rules, 78; and directed powers, 93–94; legal norms as addressed to, 39–41; and rules of recognition, 55, 56, 58, 76, 79, 81. *See also* judges/courts; legal officials
legal positivism, 8, 33, 60; and Austin, 44; and conventionalist understanding of rules of recognition, 75; and description, 110, 112, 115, 118; and Dworkin, 88, 95, 99; ethical, 111, 115–16, 121; and evaluative content, 5; of Hart, 75, 83, 110, 111; inclusive, 92–97; and judges/courts, 113, 114–15; and law as running out, 114–15; and legal validity, 4; and morality, 92–97, 109, 113–14, 115; and moral legitimacy, 121–22; and normativity, 110–15; and social facts, 4; and what law is vs. ought to be, 5
legal powers, 2
legal principles: as best possible justification, 87, 88, 89, 91–92, 107; defined, 85–87; and judicial discretion, 87, 88; and legal error, 96–97; and legal rules, 85–92; and rules of recognition, 87; and unsettled cases, 87–88

Index

legal realism, 30–33, 34
legal system, 17–19
legal validity, 2, 3–4; antireductionist
    explanation of, 19; and basic norm,
    19, 20–21, 25; conditions of, 7–8,
    126, 134; detachment from morality,
    6, 7, 14, 92, 109, 110; and efficacy,
    19; as essentially contested concept,
    134; general conditions for, 3–4, 14;
    and Hart, 35, 116; and interpreta-
    tion, 29; and Kelsen, 35; and legal
    normativity, 25; and legal system,
    18n10, 19; and morality, 4–7, 14, 88,
    92, 93, 94, 109, 110, 116; nonreduc-
    tive explanation of, 17, 35; as phase-
    sortal concept, 133; and place and
    time, 3, 19; reductive explanation of,
    28; and rules of recognition, 49–51,
    75n16, 83; and social facts, 3–4,
    24–25, 28; and social rules, 51–52;
    and sovereignty, 47; and what law
    ought to be, 69
legislature, 36, 85; and collective
    agency, 155; and compromise,
    154–55; and interpretation, 105; and
    judges, 90; and language, 154–57;
    and legislation as strategic behavior,
    154, 155–56, 157, 158
Leiter, Brian, 30, 31, 33
Lewis, David, 74, 79

MacCormick, Neil, 116n13
meaning, 15–16, 29, 99
Moore, Michael, 122
morality: and authority, 88; basic
    norm of, 27; and content of law, 67;
    and convention, 95; and Dworkin,
    95, 97, 98, 108, 110, 112; and Hart, 58,
    71, 111, 112, 116, 118, 122; and Kelsen,
    13, 14, 21, 26, 71, 109; and legal error,
    91–92; and legal norms, 61; and
    legal positivism, 92–97, 109, 113–14,
    115, 121–22; and legal principles, 85,
    87–92; and legal validity, 4–7, 88,
    93, 94, 116; legal validity detached

from, 6, 7, 14, 92, 109, 110; and
    obligation, 5–7, 71, 72; and point of
    view, 26; and rules of recognition,
    93, 94; and what law is vs. ought to
    be, 97, 98

natural law, 4–5, 25–26, 27
normal justification thesis, 64, 65, 66
norms/normativity: and Ameri-
    can legal realism, 30, 32–33; as
    authoritative instructions, 73; and
    authority, 60–73; as binding, 58;
    and commands, 38; and condi-
    tional imperatives, 27; condi-
    tions detached from content of,
    5; conflict of, 149; and conflict of
    laws, 145–46; conventional, 74; for
    creating new normative relations,
    38; and descriptive propositions,
    116–18; different types of, 41–42;
    diversity of, 88; as efficacious, 19;
    and factual aspects of law, 7–8; and
    function or purpose of law, 119–20;
    as guiding conduct, 40; and Hart,
    35, 36, 40, 48, 119; as instructions
    of some to guide conduct of others,
    67; and internal point of view, 133;
    and interpretation, 15–16, 29; and
    jurisprudence, 126; and Kelsen,
    25–27, 40, 54–55; kinds of reasons
    provided by, 5; and language,
    138–39, 140–42; and legal content,
    9; and legal positivism, 110–15; and
    legal validity, 2, 3, 4, 25, 88, 89, 133;
    legal vs. moral, 26, 27; and morality,
    6; and moral norms, 61; nonreduc-
    tive explanation of, 17; and obliga-
    tion, 57; as ought statements, 20;
    and ought vs. is statements, 17; and
    point of view, 26–28; and positive
    law, 22; as prescriptive, 1, 2; and
    Raz, 60; as reducible to one general
    form, 40–42; of relevance about
    legislative implication, 157–58; and
    rules of recognition, 81, 82, 88; and

social norms, 61; and social rules, 51–52; of strategic conversation, 158; systematic nature of, 17–19; as ultimately addressed to officials, 39–41; and valid reason for action, 25–26

obedience, 45, 46, 47, 54
obligation, 1; all-things-considered, 6; and authority, 61–62, 63–67, 70, 71; and belief, 71; and Hart, 57, 71–72; identity related, 72; and Kelsen, 26, 28; legal vs. moral, 5–7, 26, 71, 72; nature of, 2, 6; and normativity, 57; and point of view, 26, 71, 72; and power-conferring law, 39; as predictive statement of consequences, 6; and reasons for action, 65; and rules of recognition, 58, 81, 82

Perry, Stephen, 119, 122, 123
point of view, 23; grounding of, 27; internal, 53–55, 123, 130–35; and normativity, 26–28; and obligation, 26, 71, 72; and Reason, 27–28; of social rules, 53–55
positive law, 29
Postema, Gerald, 117
power, legal, 37–39
power-conferring rules, 49
pure theory of law, 8, 13

Raz, Joseph, 62; and authority, 8–9, 58, 59, 60, 61, 63–65, 69, 70, 71, 72, 83; and coercion, 42–44; and detached normative statements, 54; and Hart, 9; and inclusive legal positivism, 96; and Kelsen, 25, 26; and legal systems, 18; and morality, 93
reason/reasoning, 22; and content of law, 67; and Kelsen, 26; and legal positivism, 113; and legal principles, 85, 87–92; and point of view, 27–28; and Raz, 42, 44; and rules, 47
reasons: and authority, 70; for following rules, 57–58; identity-related,

70; for rules of recognition, 78–79; and social norms, 95
reasons for action, 1, 2, 13; and authority, 62; and conventional rules, 77, 78; identity-related, 62–63, 64, 68; and internal point of view, 130, 131, 134–35; and Kelsen, 28; and legal instructions, 143; and obligation, 65; provided by legal norms, 5; and social rules, 52, 124
reduction, 12–13, 28–34; and American legal realism, 32; and Austin, 44; and authority, 73; and Hart, 8, 35, 48, 51, 52, 53, 55, 71–72, 73, 83; and internal point of view, 131; and Kelsen, 8, 14, 15, 19, 20, 28–29, 30, 35; and legal validity, 28; and object of inquiry, 28, 29, 30; of one type of theory to another, 29–34; and relativism, 23–25; to social facts, 14–15; and social rules, 52, 53
reductive-displacement theory, 30
relativism, 22; and antireductionism, 23–25; and contingent circumstances, 24; and legal validity, 24–25
revolution, 22
rights, 2, 39
rule of law, 11
rules: about rules, 48–49; as binding/ reason-giving, 54, 55; as creating new norms or modifying existing ones, 49; as guiding conduct, 48, 49; legal, 85–92; practice theory of, 57, 58; primary, 48–49, 118; purposes of, 149, 150; reasons for following, 57–58; and regularities of behavior, 48, 54; secondary, 48–49, 56n26, 118–19. *See also* conventional rules; social rules
rules of recognition, 49–51, 60; as arbitrary, 80–81; and authority, 73–83; and the basic norm, 49–50; as compliance dependent, 80, 81; as constitutive, 82; as constitutive conventions, 79, 82; as conventions,

rules of recognition (*cont'd*)
80–82; and coordination, 78, 79, 81, 82; defined, 49; and Dworkin, 75–76, 77; hierarchical structure of, 50; and judges and other legal officials, 55–56; and legal principles, 87; and legal validity, 49–51, 75n16, 83; and morality, 93, 94; normativity of, 81, 82; and obligation, 58, 81, 82; reasons for, 78–79; and social conventions, 74–75, 95–96; and social facts, 51

sanctions, 37, 38, 40, 41–44. *See also* coercion; force
Schroeder, Mark, 24n19
social facts: and Austin, 45; and basic norm, 23–24, 25, 28; and Hart, 55, 71–72, 116; and Kelsen, 72; and legal positivism, 4; and legal validity, 3–4, 24–25, 28; reduction of law to, 14–15; and rules of recognition, 51
social norms, 61, 95
social practice, 113; and Kelsen, 19; moral vs. causal explanation of, 124–25, 126
social rules: acceptance of, 52; and authority, 73; conformity to, 52; as

constituting law, 48–59; as convention, 74; and Dworkin, 97; external point of view of, 53–54, 55; function of, 123–25; and Hart, 9, 35, 48–59; internal point of view of, 53–55; and normativity, 71; practice theory of, 52; and social conventions, 60. *See also* rules
society, function of law in, 40, 123
sovereign/sovereignty, 44–48, 57; and Austin, 35, 61; as bound by law, 67; as constituted by law, 45–46; as constituted by rules, 47–48; and habit of obedience, 46, 47, 54; and Hart, 8, 41, 45, 46, 61; as institution, 47–48; as juridical idea, 45–46; and Kelsen, 41; law as constituting, 37; law as political tool of, 36; and legal validity, 47; and rules of transition and continuity, 46–47
substantive normative legal positivism, 120–22

Thomist Natural Law, 4–5

value(s), 98; evaluation vs. understanding of, 129, 132

Waldron, Jeremy, 119, 122, 126, 127, 130

Milton Keynes UK
Ingram Content Group UK Ltd.
UKHW022159070424
440707UK00005B/252